SAINTS
A Closer Look

SAINTS:
A Closer Look

THOMAS DUBAY, S.M.

Cover design by Candle Light Studios
Cover image by Lesley Quesada
Book design by Jennifer Tibbits

LIBRARY OF CONGRESS CATALOGING-IN-PUBLICATION DATA
Dubay, Thomas.
Saints : a closer look / Thomas Dubay.
p. cm.
Includes bibliographical references (p.   ).
ISBN 978-0-86716-763-4 (pbk. : alk. paper)
1. Christian saints. I. Title.

BX2325.D84 2007
235'.2—dc22
2007025891

ISBN 978-0-86716-763-4

Published by Servant Books, an imprint of
St. Anthony Messenger Press
28 W. Liberty St.
Cincinnati, OH 45202
www.ServantBooks.org

Printed in the United States of America.
Printed on acid-free paper.
07 08 09 10 11 5 4 3 2 1

CONTENTS

A WORD OF INTRODUCTION

SAINTS ARE A REVOLUTION, PEACEFUL BUT MIGHTY. THEIR lives are not merely improvements on Aristotelian, Platonic or contemporary moral systems. Their ways of thinking and acting are not simply somewhat loftier than those of other sincere men and women. Their moral beauty is vastly more splendid. Our saints not only surpass the exhortatory descriptions of other worldviews, secular or religious. They are moral miracles far beyond the capacities of human nature left to itself.

If I were asked to describe these lofty ones in a single paragraph, I would like it to be something like the following: Saints are not only more noble and generous than the lesser of us. Each of them has had, said Saint Paul to the Ephesians, "a spiritual revolution" (4:23). They are splendid because they are profoundly in love and with no reservations, both with God and then with their families and neighbors in him. With no least desire to impress others, their heroic choices and actions flow from an inner fire, whose only source can be the Holy Spirit. And they place no impediments to its ignition. Their persevering and heroic fidelity in turn enables them to grow to their remarkable contemplative intimacies with Triune Beauty.

My hope is that examining the saints will help you and me live a full human life and achieve our own unspeakably enthralling destiny in the resurrection and the beatific vision.

PART I

Preliminary Observations

CHAPTER ONE
The Living Pinnacle

SCIENCE AND THEOLOGY INDEPENDENTLY CONVERGE IN declaring, each in its own thought patterns, that the human person is the pinnacle of visible creation. The former speaks of our brain as the most complex and amazing reality in our vast universe, far surpassing the capacities and powers of super-computers. Each cell of the trillions in our bodies is, says microbiology, as complex as a metropolitan area such as New York or Tokyo—yes, even to having computer-like technology, manufacturing capabilities and astonishingly extensive libraries of information.[1]

Our theology, deriving as it does from divine revelation, centuries ago anticipated science by extolling the human person as "little less than a god...crowned...with glory and splendour" and given dominion over all other divine works (Psalm 8:5–6). Saint John Chrysostom referred to man as "that great and wonderful living creature, more precious in the eyes of God than all other creatures!" (John Chrysostom, *Sermones in Genesim,* as quoted in *Catechism of the Catholic Church [CCC],* 358). Which is to say that we human beings are the summit of the visible cosmos. On the natural level alone we surpass in worth all the other awesome wonders that the sciences increasingly unfold before us.

Albert Einstein marveled that this universe is intelligible— that is, that it can be understood by our human minds. It is so, as Saint Thomas Aquinas noted, because creation's awesome complexities—mathematical, scientific, artistic, philosophical and theological—lie between two intellects, the divine and the human.[2]

But the splendor of the saints surpasses all these excellences of the natural order, for these glories of the Church are supernatural works of divine art. Their beauty illustrates the words of the divine Artist in Isaiah 55:8–9: "My thoughts are not your thoughts, neither are your ways my ways, says the LORD. For as the heavens are higher than the earth, so are my ways higher than your ways and my thoughts than your thoughts" *(RSV)*.

A LOOK AT EXCELLENCE

As a sort of background, we turn our attention for a few moments to the surprising differences among the saints, as indeed among all of us: the inequalities both on the natural and the supernatural levels. There are two kinds of human excellence. The first is that of talents, skills and accomplishments—for example, in scholarship, sports, music, medicine, law. It is immediately obvious that there are all sorts of degrees of gifts and achievements in these areas.

The second type of human excellence we may call personal excellence: nobility, greatness, perfection. Personal excellence is characterized by one's goodness, truth and beauty as a person—for example, in honesty, generosity, humility, chastity, selflessness, prudence and genuine love.

While individuals who have attained personal excellence are sometimes highly talented, even on occasion geniuses, most are ordinary and unremarkable in their natural gifts and accomplishments. At the same time, people who manifest the first type of excellence—that of talents, skills and accomplishments—can be far from outstanding in moral goodness. If you have some doubt about this assertion, I simply suggest that you read British historian Paul Johnson's book *Intellectuals* (Harper, 1989), a detailed study of a number of famous men and one woman who contributed to the growth of secularism by their writings and whose personal lives were morally wretched in more ways than one. Current accounts in the media of prominent sports figures, actors, entertainers, scholars, business leaders and so on who fall into serious moral aberrations are periodic reminders of this sorry reality.

The second type of human excellence is our present concern. Those who have achieved it to a heroic degree are called saints, and they are the pinnacles of human splendor.

We shall not in these pages present a series of mini-lives of these men and women. Happily we have Butler's series that does this well. We also have a large number of competent, historically accurate and well-written biographies, as well as the autobiographical classics by Saints Augustine, Teresa of Avila and Thérèse of Lisieux.

What I do plan here is expressed in the subtitle: a closer look. I shall discuss the saints' common traits and try to explain how these men and women so far surpass the lesser of us and why they are ideal models for all vocations and states in life. Here are some specific questions I plan to address:

• Participating as the saints do in our weak and wounded human nature, what makes them far better than 99 percent of people? Do their natural temperaments, strengths and weaknesses have much, if anything, to do with their rapid growth in holiness? How do the saints become the most attractive and fascinating members of our human race?

- What is the inner life of a saint like? Do saints have many temptations or severe ones? What makes them tick as men and women, as boys and girls, as teenagers? What does it mean to be head over heels in love with God?

- What does *heroic virtue* mean, and how does it come about? Is it realistic for me?

- Why and how are saints the best and most trustworthy interpreters of the gospel for the concrete details of our lives? Are they better guides than Scripture scholars?

- How and why are these men and women the surest guides out of the boredom and inner emptiness that millions of people feel in our world today? Why are the saints full of joy even in their sufferings?

- Why are the saints so immensely relevant for all of us: husbands and wives wanting to live happy family lives, bishops and priests and religious seeking to serve God and neighbor well in their consecrated vocations, single people wondering what to do with their lives?

- How do sinners, even grievous sinners, become saints? Is that transformation really possible no matter what one's past is like? If so, how can it be explained?

- What do theologians mean when they speak and write about saints as "moral miracles"? Is a moral miracle naturally impossible?

- Why do the saints have so great an impact on other people of goodwill? Is it correct to say that by and large the history of the Catholic Church is the history of her saints?

LOVERS OF GOD

It is well for us in this introductory chapter to sketch the number-one trait of these heroes and heroines of holiness: being head over heels in love with God. This American expression is strong indeed; some may think it an exaggeration. But in the remaining chapters of this work I will be spelling out the implications, conditions, requirements and unspeakable blessings that are included in this and another graphic expression: being "madly in love" with the Lord, having him as one's supreme Beloved.

The first thing to notice is that these ways of speaking are really vivid and colorful ways of talking about the greatest of all commandments (and there were six hundred–plus precepts in the Old Testament alone): to love the Lord our God with our whole heart, whole soul, whole mind and all of our strength (see Deuteronomy 6:5; Matthew 22:37). No other view of religion even comes close to this depth of intimacy with the Creator. It leaves no room for egocentrism.

As Saint John of the Cross puts it, the person in the transforming union of prayer intimacy is "lovesick" for God.[3] This is a love so mighty, so burning and so pure that it overflows into a love for neighbor that the worldly world does not even dream of, let alone live.

John, the beloved disciple, beautifully expressed this: "To love is to live according to his commandments: this is the commandment which you have heard since the beginning, to live a life of love" (2 John 1:6). As a matter of fact, each of the commandments simply spells out what real love calls for in the differing relationships and circumstances of life. Only God could have come up with this gorgeous idea, but after all, "God is love" (1 John 4:8).

The rest of this study will simply concretize and explain what living a life of genuine burning love is like. We see it first of all, of course, in Jesus himself. The Savior, tortured to death on the cross for you and me, is the perfect picture of perfect love. We see it also in his mother, whose total surrender to God opened the way to salvation. Jesus and Mary are matchless models whom saintly men and women strive with all their hearts, souls and minds to imitate.

We should not suppose that all this is easy, for the simple reason that getting rid of our embedded self-centeredness in its countless tendencies and manifestations is an arduous and uphill battle. Loving another human person is not a mere emotional feeling, not even a strong one. Nor is it a powerful attraction to a beautiful person—though many people seem to think it is.

Unless one is approaching saintliness, there is no such thing as love at first sight. There can be a mighty attraction at first sight, noble or ignoble. But attraction is not yet love. Only too often it is lust at first sight. And there is a vast chasm between real love and actual lust.

This reminds me of a psychologist's comment: "A capacity for genuine love between the sexes is rare." Not simply is the fact rare, but the capacity is rare. Apparently he was talking about the real thing, not the common media concept.

Gospel love is real: a self-giving to another even when little or nothing is received in return. It takes a great deal of deep conversion and self-sacrifice to love another person genuinely, even someone charming and winsome. Especially is this true when it is a question of growing in the totality of love or, as we have expressed it above, becoming head over heels in love.

This love is a consuming concern for the beloved's genuine welfare.

To get the feel for having God himself as our consuming concern, which is indeed a lofty sanctity, we might ask ourselves a few telltale questions:

- What do I like to do with my free time? What actually do I choose to do? Do I prefer to spend time before the television or in prayer?
- What do I like to talk about when there is someone who cares to listen? "Out of the abundance of the heart the mouth speaks" (Matthew 12:34, *RSV*).
- Am I trying seriously to be rid of my venial sins?

Progress toward God is indicated much more by actual choices than by pious feelings.

WHY BE A SAINT?

Our final purpose in this introductory chapter is to respond to two questions: Why should you read this book, and why should I bother to write it? Isn't it enough, one might say, just to squeeze into heaven? Is it that important that I strive to be a saint?

Another person may remark that, yes, the saints are undoubtedly the most beautiful women and men on our planet, but it is a hard road and a narrow gate that lead to this fullness of life and joy—and we are very weak (see Matthew 7:13–14). Can I actually do this? If so, how?

While extended answers to these questions can be found in my two works *Fire Within* (Ignatius, 1989) and *Deep Conversion/Deep Prayer* (Ignatius, 2006), I should like to offer here a few other reasons why knowing what the saints are like is of immense help in living the gospel fully in our own state of life. The rest of this book will throw more light on these observations.

1.   The incarnate Son of the Father, "the radiant light of God's glory" (Hebrews 1:3), has paid you and me the marvelous compliment of calling us to "be perfect just as your heavenly Father is perfect" (Matthew 5:48), an awesome commendation and destiny. The saints are concrete icons of what this means in priesthood, marriage, consecrated life and many different careers. They are attractive, splendid maps and living pictures showing us how specifically to imitate him who is "the Way, the Truth and the Life" (John 14:6).

2.   You and I in our various vocations will be incomparably happier precisely to the degree that we concretize and apply the gospel in our lives: "These things I have spoken to you, that my joy may be in you, and that your joy may be full" (John 15:11, *RSV*)—full, complete, not simply quite a bit. No one else promises this, and surely no one else could honor this invitation.

Yes, saints suffer as all of us do, but they suffer joyously. There is no such thing as a bored, cynical, bitter saint. If you doubt this, read the accounts of the tortures and deaths of the martyrs and the daily fidelity of all these heroines and heroes. Saint Paul, who suffered far more than most of us do (see 2 Corinthians 11:23–28), was able to say that for those who love God, all things, not just favorable and pleasant happenings, work together for good (see Romans 8:28).

3. Many, perhaps most, sufferings in the nitty-gritty of daily life are due to sin and lack of deep conversion. Mortal sins (for example, hatreds, infidelities, betrayals, divorces) devastate people, while venial sins (bickering, snapping, fighting, laziness, grouchiness, grudges, pouting and so on) multiply daily hurts and pains. Saints get over these faults, if ever they had them—another reason they find happiness in their vocation.

4. As we acquire the mind of the saints—how they look at things, how they think and make decisions—we also grow in finding solutions to the many concrete problems that books, homilies, courses and lectures by themselves cannot envision or explain fully. In other words, holiness brings a kind of light that exceeds what human words can express.

As Vatican Council II reminded us so forcefully and persuasively, the gospel calls all of us to holiness, and holiness means saintliness, not something less (see *Lumen Gentium*, 39–42; *CCC*, 2013–2014, 2028–2029). So let's take a closer look at the saints.

CHAPTER TWO
Antecedents of Holiness

IN THE CHURCH'S DEALINGS WITH EXTRAORDINARY PHENOMENA (visions, revelations, alleged miracles) through the centuries, she has consistently looked first into the natural order of the visible universe, then at times into the preternatural and finally into the supernatural. To put the matter a bit differently, when something striking or unusual occurs in human affairs, the first reaction of the Catholic Church is not to see it immediately as miraculous. That could be rash and unfounded, running contrary to our insistence on evidence before we decide matters of importance. Only when there is no possibility of explanation in the ordinary realms of human life and psychology do we turn our attention elsewhere.

In this chapter we wish to offer a thumbnail sketch of the background of heroic holiness. How do we explain the "suprahuman" goodness and beauty of the people we honor as saints? Chapters four and five of this book, on transforming intimacy with God and the consequent heroism in action, should convince each of us that of ourselves we could not live on so lofty a level over any length of time. Most would realize, I trust, that we could not do it for a week or even a day.

Now we ask what these men and women are like before there is any noteworthy sign of profound intimacy with the Trinity and heroic holiness. Is there some shared matrix or pattern in which their holiness begins and develops? Or to put the question in less technical terms, what are the saints like before they become saints? Are they at all like us lesser ones?

DIVERSITY

No one—except the Lord and his Mother, of course—has been conceived in original innocence. We will leave aside the question of Saint John the Baptist, who was filled with the Holy Spirit in the womb of his mother. Hence we may with profit ask a number of questions: What, if anything, do the natural traits and gifts of a person have to do with his or her later perfection or lack of perfection? Do physical health and strength contribute anything to the virtue of fortitude? Do the various temperaments further or hinder growth in humility, justice, patience, chastity and love? Does a high IQ add any enlightenment to the supernatural virtue of prudence?

Perhaps the most adequate answer to these inquiries is to say that natural endowments or deficiencies can contribute to the facility and ease or the difficulty and hardship in living out the various virtues, but supernatural growth is due to the grace of God, the degree of willed cooperation with that grace and the degree of conversion on the part of the person.

An individual in poor health and physically weak may be inwardly strong because of a deep and loving intimacy with the indwelling Trinity. Likewise a person of choleric temperament may have trouble with patience and humility, but a generous cooperation with grace can bring about gentleness and honesty more rapidly than for one of a mild disposition and less generosity. So also one's degree of intelligence no doubt is an asset to the infused virtue of prudence, but the fact remains that one who loves may reach supernaturally wise decisions far better than one who loves little or not at all.

Most saints are of ordinary intelligence, a goodly number very bright, a few of limited intelligence and another few geniuses. Likewise each of these men and women is a unique person, possessing a unique personality. Some are naturally charming on the human level, others less so. We need only to have studied people like Augustine, Chrysostom, Bernard, Aquinas, Teresa of Avila, John of the Cross, Philip Neri, Elizabeth Ann Seton, the Curé of Ars and Thérèse of Lisieux to appreciate how amazingly diverse these heroes and heroines of goodness can be.

We may also ask whether extraordinary favors—such as visions, private revelations and locutions—bring sanctity along with them. Once again we must make distinctions. These favors can be helpful in spurring one to greater love and effort toward sanctity, but what is more important than the favors themselves is how the recipient responds to them—that is, with what degree of love and generosity. Unusual privileges are not holiness, and a person without them may achieve a higher degree of sanctity and prayer depth than the one who does receive them. Once again, what is essential is the willed love response proved in the actions of daily life.

Then we should consider the antecedents of one's state in life, one's career, one's position in society. Do these factors make any difference in who become saints and who do not?

Those who pay close attention to the magnificent men and women we celebrate in the daily liturgies of the Church know the answers to these questions. And they who have read any substantial part of Butler's *Lives of the Saints* know even more completely, as do those who have read about the hundreds of beatifications and canonizations of recent decades.

Yes, saints are found in all races and nationalities, in all age groups: children, adolescents, young adults, mature women and men, the aged. We celebrate kings and queens as well as beggars, popes, bishops, priests, the wedded and the members of consecrated life. There are heroically holy housewives and laborers, farmers and lawyers, businessmen and medical doctors, scientists and scholars. All of them pursue their vocations assiduously and there become striking images of the unlimited Triune Beauty.

FROM SINNER TO SAINT

It may surprise some readers that I advert to the fact that the saints—again, barring Mary the Mother of God—are as naturally weak as we all are. In my youth I assumed that the saints were naturally strong, but I was wrong. In the liturgy for martyrs, those giants of fearless bravery, the Church in the Preface to the Eucharistic Prayer addresses the Lord: "You choose the weak of this world and make them strong." The saints get their new strength from the depth of their prayer lives. They are so intimately united with God that they share in his "awesome strength"—an expression Saint John of the Cross uses to describe one of the results of the transforming union, the summit of prayer growth in this life.[1]

We must go so far as to say that the ordinary saints were and are converted sinners. Some were converted from deadly, mortal sins, while all had to give up at least venial sins in a deepening conversion. Saint Mary Magdalene beautifully repented of her sinful past life. Saint Augustine gave up his sins against chastity and not only became a superbly brilliant theologian but also reached the summit of a profound contemplative intimacy with the God he loved so much. Saint Francis of Assisi overcame his wealth, worldliness and partying to become a model of voluntary poverty and of mystical depth and joy. Saint Teresa of Avila more than once regretfully spoke of her early venial sins of talking too much, having found from experience that "when words are many, transgression is not lacking" (Proverbs 10:19, *RSV*). Saint Francis de Sales so overcame his inclinations to anger that he became a model of gentleness. Saint Thérèse of Lisieux took pains to prepare herself to react lovingly when another nun would interrupt what she was doing.

Saints are like that: They do not allow even small sins to go uncorrected. With God's grace they get busy and overcome them.

From this observation of the widely differing background traits of the saints, we may draw two conclusions. One is that despite their differences, these women and men, completely free of mortal sins, are determined to correct their small ones: laziness, gossiping, grouchiness, harshness, snapping, overeating, indulgence of superfluities and wasting time with the media. They are serious about their deepening conversion. The second conclusion is that they all are entirely serious about developing intimacy with the Trinity in their meditative and contemplative prayer lives.

We proceed now to examine more closely the traits that these heroes and heroines of gospel living have in common.

CHAPTER THREE
Basic Attitudes

WE AIM IN THIS CHAPTER TO GET A FEEL FOR THE INNER thought patterns of the saints. How do they see reality and their place in it? What is their outlook on life? What are the consequences of their being so completely in love with God? Ordinary folk might put the question more prosaically: What makes them tick?

Our sketches here are purposely brief; more thorough analyses will follow in later chapters. I suggest that the reader notice and ponder the interrelationships—indeed, the intercausality—among the various traits we are discussing. They are not haphazard, just happening by chance in these remarkable men and women, as a bit of attention and active thinking will prove.

1. *God-centered.* Anyone in love, genuine love, is spontaneously focused on the beloved. God is the saints' consuming concern. While they tend to see vividly the beauties of creation and especially the preciousness of each human person, they also see everything through and in the light of the love of their lives. They live the words of the psalmist, "My eyes are always on Yahweh" (Psalm 25:15). Being in love is like that.

"What we have to do is to give up everything that does not lead to God, and all our worldly ambitions"

(Titus 2:12). This is exactly what the saints gladly do. Saint Paul expresses this trait again in one of his letters to the faithful in Corinth: "Whatever you eat, whatever you drink, whatever you do at all, do it for the glory of God" (1 Corinthians 10:31).

2. *Total.* Being thoroughly in love implies fullness of response in daily decision making. It is easy for a spouse to declare, "Darling, I love you with all my heart," but a few minutes later show grouchy impatience. That love is far from total.

It is not accidental that when Jesus proclaimed the core and greatest commandment of love, he emphasized its wholeness several times: *"You must love the Lord your God with all your heart, with all your soul, and with all your mind"* (Matthew 22:37). Corner cutting is foreign to the mind of the saint.

Saints Catherine of Sienna and Francis Xavier were windmills of work and activity on behalf of the faithful, but at prayer they were the deepest of mystics, lost in profound intimacy with their Beloved.

3. *Balanced.* One may be tempted to think that a divine focus combined with totality would yield excess in one direction or another, but such is not the case when a person's virtues have become heroic—which we will explain in chapter five. The Church will not canonize a candidate unless all the virtues are present to a heroic degree, and this requires a remarkable balance, a beautiful harmony and proportion.

Vatican Council II declared that the faithful should be "eager to act and yet devoted to contemplation, present in this world and yet not at home in it" (*Sacrosanctum Concilium*, 2). A rare beauty. Married and religious, priests and bishops, the saints give due attention to their social obligations, but they also appreciate the need for frequent periods of healthy silence. Most of them fast on occasion and are sparing at the table, and yet they eat sufficiently to maintain health. While they know that they are to live without limit the theological virtues of faith, hope and love, which aim directly at God, they are also aware that the moral virtues, which deal with created matters, are found in a mean between extremes. For them balance does not translate into mediocrity, a divided love.

4. *Determined.* Velleities, mere wishes, never produce excellence in any worthwhile human endeavor—scholarship, music, art or sports. The same is true for virtuous living— that is, personal excellence. In the spiritual life it is not enough to say, "I wish I were better," "I should improve," "I admire the saints, but...". Admiration and flabby desires get us nowhere.

    Saints say, "With God's grace I will be better, and I will begin right now. I will get rid of my vanities and my laziness. I will stop gossiping and overeating. I will stop procrastinating. I will take means to see that these changes do occur soon."

    Saint Paul was clear: "The love of Christ urges us on" (2 Corinthians 5:14, *RSV*); "I treat my body hard and make it obey me" (1 Corinthians 9:27). Without hesitation he takes the hard road and the narrow gate that open up to real happiness and an abundant life (see Matthew 7:13–14; John 10:10).[1]

5. *Dauntless in the faith.* Saints are so profoundly in love that they become fearless in the face of even extreme sufferings and sacrifices. As we have noted, they may be naturally weak, but their deep union in prayer with Divine Omnipotence gives them awesome strength. How else could we explain the burning love of Saint John de Brebeuf, who welcomed the brutal tortures and execution awaiting him at the hands of North American Indians? In his diary we read of his impassioned, fearless, love-penetrated protestations:

    > For two days now I have experienced a great desire to be a martyr and to endure all the torments the martyrs suffered.
    >
    > ...In truth I vow to you, Jesus my Savior, that as far as I have the strength I will never fail to accept the grace of martyrdom, if some day you in your infinite mercy should offer it to me, your most unworthy servant.
    >
    > ...Further, I bind myself to this so that, on receiving the blow of death, I shall accept it from your hands with the fullest delight and joy of spirit. For this reason, my beloved Jesus, and because of the surging joy which moves me, here and now I offer my blood and body and life.
    >
    > ...My God, even if all the brutal tortures which prisoners in this region must endure should fall on me, I offer myself most willingly to them and I alone shall suffer them all.[2]

6. *Utterly ecclesial.* Without exception saints have loved and do love the Church deeply, and this includes loving her

teaching, her liturgical norms and her discipline. Even in the dark days of clerical scandals, when the lives of some bishops, priests and religious were far removed from the goodness and beauty of the gospel, our heroes of holiness responded not in mediocrity but in strict adherence to magisterial doctrine and liturgical norms.

These men and women knew and lived perfectly Jesus' words about the authority of Church leaders: "Anyone who listens to you listens to me; anyone who rejects you rejects me, and those who reject me reject the one who sent me" (Luke 10:16). He made it clear likewise that he stands behind the authority of his Church until the end of the world: "And know that I am with you always; yes, to the end of time" (Matthew 28:20). He foretold that there would be scandals in his flock yet assured that the leaders would never lead the sheep astray in their binding teaching (see Matthew 16:18–19; 18:18). So it has been through the centuries.

The saints took their Lord at his word. They never left this Church he founded, nor were they even slightly inclined toward what is now called "cafeteria Catholicism," picking and choosing teachings they would accept. Never has a theological or liturgical dissenter been canonized—a simple historical fact that some of our brothers and sisters seem not to notice.

7.   *Eager for the inspired Word.* Utter faithfulness to the Church is closely allied to, indeed flows out of, a glad embrace of the biblical message. This is an ideal example of the inter-causality between these basic attitudes of the saints.

Once a month in the four-week cycle of the *Liturgy of the Hours,* we are reminded of Jeremiah 15:16: "When I found your words, I devoured them; / they became my joy and the happiness of my heart."[3] There is nothing luke-warm about the prophet's reaction to the divine Word.

Humble Teresa of Avila once remarked that she had never heard a sermon from which she did not profit. Most people would be pleased to note that they changed for the better from one homily out of ten. Heroically holy ones listen to the word of God and then get out and act on it, as Jesus admonished all of us to do (see Matthew 7:24).

8. *Joyously enthusiastic.* Saints are never bored, jaded or drift-ing. Healthy individuals in love with the Lord naturally "rejoice in the Lord always" (Philippians 4:4, *RSV*). In their freedom from egocentrism and in their God-centeredness, they experience "a joy so glorious that it cannot be described" (1 Peter 1:8). Our English word *enthusiasm* derives from the Greek word meaning "possessed by a god, having God within." Filled as the saints are "with the utter fulness of God" (Ephesians 3:19)—that is, filled with endless beauty, love and delight—it is no surprise that they do not experience boredom.

The faithful of the Old Testament were likewise thrilled with gladness in their living God (see Psalm 84:2). They pursued him with endless shouts of exultation and triumph (see Psalms 5:11; 20:5). They prayed at times with lyre and harp, string and reed, tambourine and castanet, beating of drums, clashing of cymbals and dancing as well (see Psalms 87; 149; 150; 2 Samuel 6:5). (If he who sings in worship prays twice, perhaps these dancing people were praying thrice!)

Nothing dreary or dull here: God was in their midst. This enthusiasm was not a mere emotional experience, though feelings can be a natural overflow. And we should note that this great delight in God is compatible with disappointments and sufferings—which suggests the next basic outlook of the supernaturally transformed person.

9. *Welcoming the cross.* Even though the saints, like the rest of us, feel a natural repugnance toward suffering (as did Jesus himself in his agony in the garden), they nonetheless generously embrace the hardships that come their way in daily life (see Luke 9:23). They likewise go out of their way to fast prudently on occasion and otherwise to chastise their bodies, to correct what is amiss in their behavior (see again 1 Corinthians 9:27).

    Saint Paul was so enamored of the Lord's cross and his share in it that he wanted to know only Jesus and him crucified (see 1 Corinthians 2:2). Loving to share in the Lord's passion is deeply engrained in the outlook of the saints.

10. *Intellectual and academic honesty.* More than a few readers may be surprised at this saintly trait and the extended attention I give it in chapter seven. Most of us assume that scholars are honest in their thinking, speaking and writing. I should like to think that most are, but experience over the years in both scientific and theological fields indicates not a few exceptions. Especially is this the case when the two have common concerns.

    Let it be said here that the saints are among those to whom we can look for the truth. There are many scholarly saints who have devoted their intellects and their lives to contesting heresy and expounding truth. Of particular note are the giants of the patristic age—such as Augustine, Athanasius and John Chrysostom; the medieval greats— Albert, Thomas, Bonaventure and Robert Bellarmine; and their noncanonized associates—such as Cajetan, Suarez and the Spanish Salmanticenses.

We also find this intellectual honesty in the under-appreciated manuals of moral theology common in the twentieth century. These authors assumed as obvious that objections are to be faced and given competent responses. Nothing was to be covered over.

11. *Logically consistent.* For many people, even religiously-minded ones, there is a considerable gap, sometimes size-able, between what they profess in their prayers and what they actually do in practice. It is easy for a man to say in his prayers, "Lord, I love you with all my heart," and a few minutes later prove that his heart is divided by eating too much, watching useless television or snapping at his wife. Or a woman may avow in her morning devotions, "I want to love my neighbor as myself," and later engage in gossip or grouchiness. The same inconsistencies occur among members of consecrated life and among the clergy.

Not so with the saints. What they profess they live. When they hear or read that deep intimacy with God is the "one thing," the top priority in life, they decide to make meditative and contemplative prayer a daily practice. When they realize that God is himself endless delight, a delight he wants to share with us, they make up their minds to give up everything that does not lead to him— just as Saint Paul told all of us to do (see Philippians 3:8).

When the saints sit down to dinner, they choose what they eat and drink for his glory (and their own welfare), not merely to flatter their palates (see 1 Corinthians 10:31). Saints shed wiggle room in living out the gospel, and they leave no place for pseudorationalizations.

12. *On fire*. In the recorded words of Jesus, we are continually surprised and challenged, even taken aback, at how completely original and unconventional he is. His thoughts are indeed revolutionary, and at the same time serious reflection shows them to be true, right on target. God always gets it right. Among these stimulating, provocative bolts from the blue we hear him say, "I came to cast fire upon the earth; and would that it were already kindled!" (Luke 12:49, *RSV*). There is nothing bland or banal in that idea, and who else would ever say so colossal a thing?

The saints do burn, and they radiate at times. When Saint Philip Neri celebrated Mass, he would experience what Vatican Council II said about our being aflame with love during the liturgy (see *Sacrosanctum Concilium,* 10). On occasion this priest's intense love prevented him from saying the words of the Mass; he had to pause for up to two hours to recover his capacity to speak.

Witnesses for the canonization process of Saint Teresa of Avila testified that when she received the Eucharist, her face visibly radiated joy. The Lord was casting fire on the earth. Which reminds us of the comment of the two disciples on the road to Emmaus after the risen Lord had left them: "Did not our hearts burn within us as he talked to us on the road and explained the scriptures to us?" (Luke 24:32).

13. *Fully alive.* If we reflect on the inner traits we have sketched in this chapter, we may be led to summarize them in one expression: "living life to the hilt." Because of their deep conversion and profound intimacy with the Trinity, the saints' human potentials are fulfilled as far as they can be this side of the beatific vision: knowing, loving, delighting. *"The things that no eye has seen and no ear has heard, things beyond the mind of man, all that God has prepared for those who love him"* (1 Corinthians 2:9).

This is of one piece with Jesus' explanation of why he appeared on our earth: "I have come so that they may have life and have it to the full" (John 10:10). In the third century Saint Irenaeus proclaimed that a man alive is a glory to God.[4] Such are the saints.

PART II
The Intercausal Core

CHAPTER FOUR
Transforming Intimacy

WE COME NOW TO THE BASIC CORE AND INNER DYNAMO OF saintliness. We look into the deep energy within that drives all else in these remarkable women and men. It calls for a somewhat extended treatment.

There are two basic aspects of any authentic human life. On the one hand we engage in visible, external activities: speaking, working, moving about, recreating, studying and a host of others. On the other hand we experience and express interpersonal sentiments toward the people dear to us and toward what should be the central love in our lives, God. Cast in theological terms of our supreme vocation, the call to the beatific vision, the two basic aspects of a healthy human existence are action and contemplation.

These two dimensions of our lives are not simply juxtaposed but are inwardly related to each other: external activities are rooted in fundamental love relationships. Saint Paul referred to this inner orientation when he admonished the Corinthians that whatever they were doing—whether eating, drinking or anything else—it was to be directed to the glory of God (see 1 Corinthians 10:31). Vatican Council II made this point when it declared that for all of us, action is to be subordinated and directed to contemplation (see *Sacrosanctum Concilium*, 2).

So it is with holiness: There are two aspects, two sides, to becoming a saint: our everyday activities and our growing intimacy with the Trinity. These two sides have been expressed through the centuries in various ways. The psalmist can simply remark, "Praise comes well from upright hearts" (Psalm 33:1)—that is, the person who lives virtuously will have an authentic prayer life. More explicit still is the statement "The close secret of Yahweh belongs to them who fear him" (Psalm 25:14)—that is, to those who keep his word. A footnote to this text in the *Jerusalem Bible* comments: "Not so much the mystery of God himself, Wisdom 2:22, as an intimacy with God, Psalm 73:28."

Jesus, in linking the two most important commandments, brings out this double aspect of holiness: a total love for God and the demonstration of this love in caring for our neighbors (see Matthew 22:34–40). Hence the core of lofty holiness has two tightly intertwined aspects: a transforming intimacy in prayer and a consequent heroism in action, as one extends that love to the brothers and sisters of the incarnate Word.

Jesus put the matter in still another way: If we want to live totally with full joy, we are going to have to take the hard road and the narrow gate (see Matthew 7:13–14). Supreme life is a deep interpersonal union with endless Beauty. Now, this oneness is impossible unless we are purified from our egocentrisms in our daily decisions and choices—which is indeed a hard road to take, but it does lead to abiding joy in this world and to eternal enthrallment in the next.

Saint Augustine neatly put all this in a few words when he remarked that to pray well we must live well. That is, to grow in prayer depth we must practice all the virtues: patience, humility, obedience, chastity, honesty and all the rest. The opposite causality is also the case: to live well one must pray well. That is, living the virtues generously is greatly furthered by prayer intimacy. Truth is symphonic. Authentic holiness is beautiful. The indwelling Father, Son and their Holy Spirit become a growing, inner-energizing source, and from this fortifying fountain flow exteriorly apparent results.

In the rest of this chapter we shall consider the first aspect, which is the root of saintliness, a transforming intimacy with God himself. In our next chapter we shall discuss heroic virtue. Together these two sides of holiness make up the moral miracle that is a saint.

THE QUESTION OF AUTHENTICITY

First we raise a reality issue. Is there such a thing as real intimacy with God? Can the Trinity, who is endlessly beyond anything and everything created, actually be experienced in an inter-personal union? In this life no one can possibly see the Lord as he is in himself. How could we be intimate? What are we to think of the alleged experiences of God that we read about in well-researched and sober biographies of Augustine, Bernard, Aquinas, Bonaventure, Catherine of Siena, Teresa of Avila, John of the Cross and others? Is it God they meet, or are we dealing with the emotional imaginings of enthusiastic people?

This book is not aimed at proving its premises at length, though in this case that could be done without much trouble. A few brief observations are in order.

We have already shown in the previous chapter that the saints who speak (almost always reluctantly) of their experiences of God are people of impeccable honesty and integrity.

The public media periodically remind us of lapses in candor among celebrities and even in the professions and the academic community. I have found throughout my adult life of study that the saints are far more reliable in what they report than a disturbing number of secular authors and speakers. The saints face facts and are not at all inclined to cover up what does not seem to fit their theses.

A second observation: Yes, there are people who mistakenly think they are in contact with God but actually are not. There are ways of discerning the invalidity of their notions. These erroneous claims have existed in the past and still exist in the present, but I am not speaking about them here. This is a book about the saints, in the present context including intellectually brilliant men and women.

What Saint Teresa of Avila describes in her autobiography and in her spiritual testimonies (both humbly written in obedience) could not be imagined in their power and beauty. If one doubts this statement, I would suggest he or she read these two works with an open mind. Atheist intellectual and scholar Edith Stein read the autobiography in one long nocturnal session. When she put the book down, she declared, "This is the truth!"[1] She had an open mind and good sense. Not surprisingly, she entered the Church and became one of Teresa's nuns—and a saint.

Our best scientists and our finest theologians are of one mind that the beauty of a theory, equation or idea is the best evidence that it is true.[2] That is the way the universe and the supernatural order are set up. As a philosopher would put it, truth, goodness and beauty are transcendental properties of being. The splendor of both the saints themselves and what they narrate of their advanced experiences of God amply fulfills this criterion of truth.

Furthermore, genuine contacts with God are usually independent of antecedents—that is, of what the recipients are thinking about or desiring. They are unexpected, often surprising and on occasion flatly contrary to what the person assumes. They are often unforgettable and indelible. Mere emotions have none of these traits.

One final observation regarding this question of authenticity: My own experience with many deeply sincere and intelligent people provides repeated evidences that their prayer lives are real, beyond invention. The many ways in which men and women who have read nothing of the mystics and yet converge in describing what is actually indescribable is proof positive that they are indeed in touch with the real and only God. The heroic level of their daily lives usually confirms this fact. These are the most credible people on the planet.

GROWING INTIMACY

We are now prepared to sketch what this transforming intimacy with the Lord is actually like. But first of all we note what it is not.

We do not envision here extraordinary phenomena, though God does offer these when he chooses. We are not considering therefore visions and revelations, locutions or the experience of fragrances. These are not necessary for holiness. Nor are we discussing emotions that can arise from natural causes, such as seeing one's human beloved after a long absence or the sense pleasures of eating and drinking. Nor is this an impersonal, loveless, oriental awareness. Finally this encounter is not experienced via images, ideas and concepts.

How then shall we describe an intimacy with the living God, who can ordinarily be neither seen nor touched in this life? In its advancing stages it is an experienced interpersonal closeness that he gives and the individual human receives—which is why we speak of it as "infused."

My experience in thousands of spiritual direction chats makes clear that there are numberless manners and degrees in which the Lord communicates his closeness. Yes, there can be an overflow into the recipient's sense life, an emotional overflow, but in itself the intimacy is beyond images, ideas and concepts. This is why theologians call it dark—that is, unlike our ordinary ways of knowing things.

The intimacy with Christ is of many differing types: desiring, thirsting, yearning, knowing, delighting, loving. There are also numberless degrees of intensity: a gentle, loving awareness; a pleasant seeking; a strong yearning; an absorbing delight, free of distractions; a burning love; an ecstatic joy. There are many fluctuations in a growing life of contemplative intimacy—in degrees of intensity, types of intimacy and duration. These variations, of course, make clear who is in charge; it is obvious that the recipient is not causing the experience.

Anyone who has prayed the Psalter for long is aware of its numerous mentions of these encounters with God. They are meant for everyone. We are to grow to the point where our minds are always on the Lord (see Psalm 25:15)—a lofty degree of intimacy not naturally attainable. One growing in this closeness can "taste" the divine goodness and become radiant with joy (see Psalm 34:5, 8). This individual's heart and flesh, his very being, sing with delight to the living God (see Psalm 84:2).

Even when the Lord seems absent, he can give a thirst for himself beyond the human capacity to produce. The recipient of this experience may be led to sing through the night of the God of his life. Yearning for his Maker, he meditates on him all night long (see Psalms 42:1–2, 8; 63:1, 6).

This passage reminds us that—while attentive vocal prayer is a beginning in the process of drawing close to God—meditating on his word, with its inner conversation with him, is a deepening of this closeness. It is significant that the first two verses of the inspired book of prayer make the point that the person who ponders the divine Word day and night is happy and flourishes (see Psalm 1:1–2). Then when one is ready for a still deeper communing, the Lord begins to give the intimacy of which we are presently speaking, contemplative prayer, with a growth even to its summit.

At the Last Supper, while Jesus was discoursing about the indwelling Trinity, he spoke of our knowing the Holy Spirit because he is in us and with us. For the Hebrew mind, to "know" another person involves an experience of that person. Thus to know God indwelling means to experience the Father, Son and Holy Spirit, which itself is a transforming intimacy (see John 14:15–17). In his first letter Saint Peter speaks to the faithful of a profound delight that they have received, so deep that it cannot be put into words; it is inexpressible (see 1 Peter 1:8). Peter adds that we taste the very goodness of this Triune Beauty dwelling within us (see 1 Peter 2:3, alluding to Psalm 34:8).

FILLED WITH FULLNESS

The greatest of all the commandments, an entirely total love for God, is of course the most sublime degree of intimacy with him (see Luke 10:27). When Saint Paul explains to the Ephesians the matchless and limitless love of Christ for us, he declares that in receiving it they are to be "filled with the utter fullness of God" (Ephesians 3:19). In the same verse he notes that this interpersonal closeness surpasses all knowledge. Indeed, it surpasses all possible experiences.

Not surprisingly the early patristic giants—Augustine, Gregory of Nyssa and John Chrysostom—speak in the same vein. The last named, for example, eloquently explains to his flock what this sublime intimacy is like. In the fifth century this marvelous bishop, himself burning with love, urged his people to a loving longing too deep for words, a profound prayer that humans cannot produce but only receive from the Holy Spirit. These longings are inexpressible, and "one who tastes this food is set on fire.... His spirit burns as in a fire of the utmost intensity."[3] We should notice that the Church, in placing part of this homily in the *Liturgy of the Hours*, is showing that this profound contemplative prayer is meant for everyone.

The biblical and ecclesial tradition continues in the medieval theologians and saints, such as Bernard, Francis of Assisi, Thomas Aquinas, Bonaventure and Catherine of Siena. Bonaventure, in his *Soul's Journey into God,* writes, "No one receives except him who desires it, and no one desires except him who is inflamed in his very marrow by the fire of the Holy Spirit."[4]

In the same work this Franciscan theologian writes of the mind's ascending "through wonder to wondering contemplation"[5] and of "the fire that totally inflames and carries us into God by ecstatic unctions and burning affections."[6] And referring to the very heights of divine intimacy on earth, Bonaventure tells us that

> new, absolute and unchangeable mysteries of theology
> are hidden
> in the superluminous darkness
> of a silence
> teaching secretly in the utmost obscurity
> which is supermanifest—
> a darkness which is super-resplendent
> and in which everything shines forth
> and which fills to overflowing.[7]

In a manner reminding us of Saint Paul's words to the Ephesians (noted above), we find here a fullness that fulfills our every capacity—an astonishing reality. "In God alone there is primordial and true delight and...in all of our delights we are led to seek this delight."[8]

Saint Francis of Assisi is known even in the secular world for his extraordinary joy, a joy that included a delight in creation as so many sparklings pointing to the unlimited beauty of and delight in the Creator. This dimension of transforming intimacy Bonaventure touches upon in his *Life of Saint Francis:*

> Like a glowing coal,
> he seemed totally absorbed
> in the flame of divine love....
> In beautiful things
> he saw Beauty itself
> and through his *vestiges* imprinted on creation
> *he followed his Beloved* everywhere,
> making from all things a ladder

by which he could climb up
and embrace him *who is utterly desirable.*
With a feeling of unprecedented devotion
he savored
in each and every creature—
as in so many rivulets—
that Goodness
which is their fountain-source.[9]

It would be difficult to express more adequately the exquisite harmony that should prevail in our human reactions to creation and its Creator. Not only should there be no least clash between the two, but the one is meant to lead to the other. Truth is indeed symphonic.

Saint John of the Cross, prince of mystics, has given us what could be termed "gem definitions" of Christic contemplation. He refers to differing types and degrees of intensity in the various ways the Lord communicates himself to those who serve him with growing generosity. Typical of the expressions we find sprinkled through John's work are "loving knowledge," "spiritual light," "ray of darkness," "unintelligible peace," "loving light and wisdom," "loving fire of contemplation," "this purgative and loving knowledge," "burning of love," "wondrous wisdom," "loving inflow of God."[10]

We should notice how profoundly interpersonal these gems are. In fact it is precisely because they are so interpersonally intimate that they are transformative. These experiences have almost nothing in common with the impersonality of Buddhist awareness and New Age eclectic superficialities. Saints are exciting for many reasons, one of which is that they are so real.

TRANSFORMING UNION

We are now ready to look more closely at the gradual unfolding of this divine-human communion until it reaches its summit. Like any lofty human intimacy, intimacy with God is not a sudden achievement.

In the created order beautiful realities grow gradually from an incipient beginning, through intermediate stages and into the final splendid fullness. A majestic oak tree begins as an acorn. Gorgeous tulips, orchids and grains of wheat begin as bulbs and seeds, and then they become tiny green shoots breaking through the dark earth into bright sunlight. Only in their full blossoming do they express their consummate glory.

Except for the Mother of God, the most favored among women from the moment of her conception (see Luke 1:28, 42), saintliness is no exception to the rule we see in the natural order. It begins, of course, with baptism and is nourished by the vocal prayers we learn as children and by our participation in the sacramental life of the Church. It grows also to the extent that we get rid of our egocentrisms: petty clingings, vanities, gossip, laziness, overeating, quarreling, pouting, grouchiness, snapping at people, wasting time, small dishonesties.[11] This growing closeness to God leaps notably forward when we embrace a serious and habitual meditative prayer life, which increases our capacity for a still deeper intimacy. Then God begins to give us the new kind of prayer we call *contemplation*.[12]

This discussion of contemplative intimacy with the indwelling Trinity may require patient thought because this intimacy is so sublime and, as a matter of fact, not common—even though every one of us is called to its heights.[13] Patient

pondering is in order also because this subject is rarely mentioned, let alone adequately explained, in the thousands of
religious books that pour out of our publishing houses each
year. Nor do we hear of it on Sunday mornings from the pulpit, even though God's Word and the Church's magisterial
teaching clearly present it in the liturgy and in the saints the
Church canonizes. The matter is actually beautifully simple.
Returning to Paul's words to the Ephesians, we are to be
"filled with the utter fulness of God" (Ephesians 3:19).

Yet we may have a problem with believability. Some people may assume that we are overstating the reality, indulging
in hyperbole. In our contemporary society we are so weary of
overblown advertising, assertions and political oratory that
we are automatically suspicious of what can seem to be
inflated language and extravagant claims. Yet the fact remains
that what I write about here is now happening in our world.
I am not speaking about visions or apparitions but about
something far more important.

The transforming union with God is the deepest root of
holiness, the summit of what human life on earth is meant to
be in the mind of the supreme Artist. This oneness with him
is the normal preparation here below for the final and
unspeakable intimacy of the beatific vision. The supreme
Artist is also obviously the supreme Optimist.

This final peak of prayer intimacy with the indwelling
Trinity is the summit from which a person can live all the
virtues heroically. As we have noted, it is not a sudden happening, a "big bang" in our life with God. Saint Teresa details
its gradual growth in the seven mansions of her *Interior
Castle*.[14]

What type of union is this? As Saint John of the Cross explains, this summit is a knowing-loving-delighting union with Father, Son and Holy Spirit. There is a remarkable oneness of intellects and wills, divine and human. The recipient has a divinizing but non-pantheistic likeness to the Trinity. No selfish clingings remain; rather there is a purity from anything ungodly. The disciple enjoys a deep knowing of the indwelling Trinity, unlike anything experienced before in study or in prayer.

Saint Paul prays that the Colossians "through perfect wisdom and spiritual understanding" should reach the fullest knowledge of the divine will, and so come to lead the kind of life the Lord expects of them, a "life acceptable to him in all its aspects" (Colossians 1:9–10). How more lofty could one get on this side of the beatific vision? The apostle remarks to the Ephesians that God has richly graced them "in all wisdom and insight" (Ephesians 1:8).

Understandably this remarkable knowledge is accompanied by perfect love and delight. Here we turn to John of the Cross, a master of explaining in metaphorical language what cannot be expressed adequately in literal terms: "God himself is for [the soul] many lamps together. They illumine and impart warmth to it individually, for it has clear knowledge of each [divine attribute], and through this knowledge is inflamed in love.... All these lamps are one lamp, which according to its powers and attributes shines and burns like many lamps."[15]

What is John saying here? The pondering I mentioned above is much in order. A lamp of fire, light and love represents one of the divine attributes, such as goodness, power, joy, wisdom, tenderness or purity. And each attribute (lamp) thrills and enkindles the recipient, and it bestows remarkably new insight and a keen delight with burning love. Furthermore, says the saint in another place, the person is *within* these beauties and is transformed *in* them. One is enthralled within each of the divine splendors.

I would add a note from my earlier work *Fire Within:* "Even though all the divine attributes [beauties] are utterly one in God, each of them is seen and enjoyed distinctly, and each enlightens the others."[16] Indeed, in our wildest imaginings we could not suspect what God has prepared for those who love him—even in this world (see 1 Corinthians 2:9).

In this connection Saint John of the Cross speaks of an experience known to other Christian mystics as well—namely, "the intimate spiritual embrace." There is no doubt that this is more than an earthly cuddle, squeeze or clasp, but we have no choice but to use familiar terms. This supernatural hug can be so strong "that the soul needs an infusion of special strength to endure it."[17]

UNION'S RESULTS

My next task is to sketch some of the effects of this remarkable union. The first is that the person experiences a continuing, abiding awareness of the Lord indwelling. In lesser degrees of infused contemplation, this awareness is interrupted by distractions and the ordinary activities of daily life, but at the summit there is an habitual experience of God that persists along with attention to other occupations. This can be called a dual awareness. Hence the recipient can be conversing with another person, teaching a class or caring for a baby at home on one undiminished level of awareness and at the same time, on a deeper level, experience a delightful inner presence of the Lord.

In this transforming union there are on occasion more intense bursts of love that are not continual. John of the Cross aptly explains that these two modes of union are "like the difference between the wood on fire and the flame leaping up from it, for the flame is the effect of the fire present there."[18]

A second result of this seventh mansion (Saint Teresa of Avila's terminology) is that disordered and excessive tendencies disappear or are greatly diminished. For example, the person lives completely Saint Paul's advice to the Corinthians to do all for the glory of God, not to flatter unredeemed inclinations (see 1 Corinthians 10:14–33). Inner turmoil ceases, and a serene harmony and calm accompany the inner love and delight.

A cessation of inner suffering is the third consequence. The reason for this is that there now remains nothing to be purified, no abiding selfishness to cause inner pain. Outer sufferings may continue—such as illness, hurts from others, hot or cold weather—but these and other crosses are borne with joy, even with delight. The painful longings for the Beloved in the previous purifying nights of dark prayer are likewise gone: The Lord is now continually experienced.

In this "spiritual marriage," still another name for this summit of intimacy, it follows also that the person is loving God and others in everything that happens, whether it be painful or delightful. This is of one piece with what Saint John the Evangelist wrote of in his second letter: "The commandment which you have heard since the beginning [is] to live a life of love" (2 John 6). Life becomes loving. What could be more beautiful, more divine? Which, of course, is why a saint rejoices in the Lord always (see Philippians 4:4), whether in

prosperity or in pain, whether working or recreating or praying. As we must note again, no other worldview comes
close to this.

The fifth result of this summit is more difficult to explain;
we may call it "coacting with God." The union with him is now
so intensely close that the person is keenly sensitive to the
direction of the Holy Spirit (see Romans 8:14) and acts with
the Spirit in a highly intimate manner. At this stage of growth
the saint's first inclinations, even before his will is operating,
are inclined toward the divine. For example, when mistreated
by another individual, his or her first reaction—before reasoned thought occurs—is one of love. This is being led by the
Spirit in a lofty manner.

Trait number six is likewise wondrous: a fresh new delight
in created beauty, a thrilling enjoyment far beyond what a
mere naturalist would experience. The saint enjoys so intimate
a communion with the divine Artist that a new and primal
radiance is shed on a leaf, a rose, a snowflake, a lovely face—
and most especially on the soul behind the face.

My sketches here of the results of the transforming summit of prayer are brief. I have written more extensive explanations, including the biblical bases for these traits, in my book
Fire Within, chapter ten. Of course, John of the Cross gives the
most complete account in his *Spiritual Canticle* and *Living
Flame of Love.*

Our next chapter on heroism in action is a fuller treatment
of how the primal source of virtue is made visibly manifest in
the lives of the saints. John of the Cross indicates these two
sides of holiness—the one flowing from the other, the visible
from the invisible—when he speaks of "a singular fortitude

and a very sublime love...needed for so strong and intimate an embrace from God.... The soul obtains not only a very lofty purity and beauty but also an amazing strength [to live heroically well] because of the powerful and intimate bond effected between God and her by means of this union."[19]

CHAPTER FIVE
Heroic Virtue in Action

BEFORE WE PLUNGE IN THIS CHAPTER INTO THE DEPTHS OF human personal excellence and what it may involve, we must be clear about what we in our Catholic theology understand the virtues to be and not to be. We begin with the latter.

The virtues—personal goodness, sanctity—do not consist in mere external manners, proprieties or etiquette. (Someone has remarked that etiquette is the morality of the irreligious.) The virtues go way beyond formal routine and loveless conformities. Inner authenticity is paramount in Christ-centered morality.

Nor are the virtues natural inclinations—for example, to gentleness or silence. A proclivity is not meritorious until it is embraced or acted upon with free will and for the right motivation. Similarly a natural bent toward harshness is not blameworthy until a free decision comes into play and prompts the rough treatment of another person.

In broad terms we may define the virtues as the fulfillment of our human potentials or capacities. By living them the person progressively becomes more and more human and even divinized, ever closer to what we are meant to be in the divine plan. Each virtue is a power to embrace the true, the good and the beautiful in one way or another. Each of them is an aspect of full Christlike humanness. Each is a power by which a person becomes more complete as a man or a woman: loving, humble, patient, chaste, generous. Or to speak in New Testament terms, living the virtues is doing the will of the heavenly Father in all the sundry details of daily life (see, for example, Mark 3:35; John 5:30; 6:38; Ephesians 5:15–20). And his will is always for our own greater good.

In more precise theological terms, a virtue is a good quality, perfection or habit by which a person acts in a manner that makes him or her a better person—not merely talented, skilled, gifted or accomplished. A virtue is called "natural" or "acquired" when the habit results from our own worthy actions; when the power comes directly from God without any effort on our part, it is called "infused."

Moral virtues are concerned with created realities—for example, temperance and justice—whereas the three theological virtues deal immediately with God: Faith means saying yes to the Trinity and to their divine message; hope is our expectation of heaven and trust in the divine promises and the grace to get there; charity is the virtue "by which we love God above all things for his own sake, and our neighbor as ourselves for the love of God" (see *CCC*, 1812–1829). As we live the virtues in our action and contemplation, work and prayer, each of us is becoming more and more like the Master. "We are God's work of art, created in Christ Jesus to live the good life as from the beginning he had meant us to live it" (Ephesians 2:10).

As we have noted above, God does not ask for mere external appearances of right doing. Jesus vigorously condemned such pretense in the Pharisees (see Matthew 23:23). It seems that many people assume that their actions are right and pleasing to God: "A man's conduct may strike him as pure, Yahweh, however, weighs the motives" (Proverbs 16:2). Our motivation must proceed from love and unfeigned faith, free of pretense. We are to love one another sincerely (see 2 Corinthians 6:6; 1 Peter 1:22). We must pray, fast and live righteously for the right reasons, not to be admired or merely to lose weight (see Matthew 5:46; 6:1–6; 16–18). Right motivation is immensely important, and so is the degree of love that prompts our actions.

WHEN ARE THE VIRTUES HEROIC?

We are now ready to raise the next logical question: When do the virtues reach the pinnacle of their development?

We begin with the inspired Word. Sacred Scripture calls all of us to a lofty, perfect holiness. The saints are men and women who say a complete yes to this call, not merely in prayerful sentiments but also in daily decisions and actions. The psalmist seeks the Lord with his whole heart, not with 85 or 98 percent of it (see Psalm 119:10), and his mind is always on his God, not simply during the liturgy and private prayers (see Psalm 25:15).

In the Sermon on the Mount Jesus admonishes us to "be perfect as [our] heavenly Father is perfect" (Matthew 5:48). We cannot imagine a loftier holiness. Further on the Lord tells us that our love for God is to be so great that he emphasizes its totality no less than four times in one sentence: with our whole heart, whole soul, whole mind and all our strength. Then he adds the superhuman admonition that we love our neighbors as we love ourselves (see Luke 10:27).

Saint Paul teaches us that we are to do everything for the glory of God—which of course is also for our own good (see

1 Corinthians 10:31). In the divine plan there is to be in us no lukewarmness, no mediocrity. We are to live in a way that our God may call perfect, and if we do not, the solution is one word: repent (see Revelation 3:2–3).

We may round out this charming description of heroic holiness with Saint Paul's challenge to the Ephesians: before the world was made, God chose us in his Son "to be holy and spotless, and to live through love in his presence" (Ephesians 1:4). Spotless, no less!

The saints work assiduously to rid themselves of the many defects that reside in most people throughout their lives: excessive desires for esteem, eating too much or too avidly, indulging in comfort to the neglect of duty, showing impatience, petty attachments to a type of recreation or to a particular television program, procrastination, exaggerations in speech, wasting time through idle chatter or excessive amusements, omissions of all sorts (a smile, a word of commendation, a helping hand), mixed motivation, petty vanities. Freeing the self of these and similar faults is to advance progressively closer to being "holy and spotless." The saints operate in just this fashion because they are totally in love with their supreme Beloved.

We may encapsulate the theological concept of heroic holiness with two representative sentences from our centuries-old tradition. First, Saint Thomas Aquinas pointed out that ordinary virtues bring a person to perfection in a human manner, but heroic virtues do so in a superhuman manner. Second, Pope Benedict XIV stated, in his several-volume work on the beatification and canonization of saints, that the nature of heroic virtue is a height of perfection that far surpasses the goodness of ordinary people who, although they are in a state of grace, put less effort toward Christian perfection.

The richness of these two theological formulations can be seen in the traits of heroic holiness we now move on to examine. How do the saints live day by day? What determines their thinking and aspirations, their choices and actions?

SAYING YES TO GOD

The very taproot of all heroic virtues is the intensity of the personal yes to God in the theological virtues of faith, hope and love. The saint's love-penetrated embrace of the Father, Son and Holy Spirit and of their Triune revelation is far stronger than that of the ordinary faithful, who also say yes but with less depth, vivacity and eagerness. So also the saint's trust in receiving everything needful for the attainment of the beatific vision in the risen body far surpasses in intensity that of lesser souls.

The strength of this triple faith-hope-love yes to God is primarily a matter of will, though often there is a notable emotional overflow. In any event it is not a mere sentiment but is proved to be genuine in daily choices and actions: in remarkable patience, sacrifice, obedience, fortitude and all the other moral virtues. This core trait of intensity appears frequently in the New Testament: in the Mother of the Lord, Saint Paul and the other apostles after Pentecost, Mary Magdalene after her conversion, Stephen and so on. Here are a few concrete examples from three later saints.

Many readers of these pages most likely have read of Saint Augustine's profound love-yes to God in his classic *Confessions*. I here offer a few illustrations from his lesser-known masterpiece *The Trinity*. Augustine's biblical and theological explorations in this long study are wondrously acute, groundbreaking and brilliant—and he had no help from computer software or concordances!

Augustine burned to know more and more deeply the inexpressible truth of Triune Beauty. He closed this long and arduous work with a lengthy prayer to God. We may be content here with a small sampling from it:

> I have sought you and desired to see intellectually what I have believed, and I have argued much and toiled much. O Lord my God, my one hope, listen to me lest out of weariness I should stop wanting to seek you, but let me seek your face always, and with ardor. Do you yourself give me the strength to seek, having caused yourself to be found and having given me the hope of finding you more and more. Before you lies my strength and my weakness; preserve the one, heal the other. Before you lies my knowledge and my ignorance; where you have opened to me, receive me as I come in; where you have shut to me, open to me as I knock. Let me remember you, let me understand you, let me love you. Increase these things in me until you refashion me entirely.[1]

Our second example of this heroism in the theological virtues is Saint Teresa of Avila. She was a woman head over heels in love in her God-penetrated world, and yet at the same time she gave herself unstintingly to others. This care for her neighbor was obvious in her voluminous correspondence—she wrote letters until one or two in the morning, rising a few hours later for early community prayer—and in her tending to menial tasks in the monastery. To see this firsthand the reader only need peruse some typical pages of her works.

Teresa said of herself—and it was noted in the canonization process—that she never had a temptation against faith. She had fallen in love with "His Majesty," and clinging to his word was no problem to her. This yes in faith, hope and love was the root of her astonishing trust in the care of Divine Providence. Her life is full of examples of how impossibilities became possible. Bearing this in mind, we understand why she found timid people "oppressive."[2]

Teresa's superior directed her to write, and when she did, professions of her great love for the Lord of her life spontaneously burst forth from her mind and her pen. These brief prayers can be found frequently in her writings; several examples from her *Soliloquies* will suffice for our purposes: "O life, life! How can you endure being separated from your Life?"[3] She goes on to describe God as "My Lord and my delight.... Cure for anyone who wants to be cured by You.... O my delight.... My Glory.... My Good.... O compassionate and loving Lord of my soul.... O Life, who gives life to all.... O gentle Repose of my God's lovers.... O my Happiness and my God.... My rest from all pains.... My Spouse, ...my true Lover."[4]

At slightly greater length Teresa reflects her longing for her Spouse, and at the same time she grants us a peek into why prayerful intimacy was so precious to her: "I often reflect, my Lord, that if there is something by which life can endure being separated from You, it is solitude."[5] Finally, a glimpse into the fire that burned in the foundress's heart: "Since *my Beloved is for me and I for my Beloved*, who will be able to separate and extinguish two fires so enkindled? It would amount to laboring in vain, for the two fires have become one."[6] These words speak for themselves.

I do not multiply examples unduly in adding one from another woman burning with love, another doctor of the Church, Saint Catherine of Siena. The Church has seen fit to include this quote in celebrating her feast day in the *Liturgy of the Hours*. Addressing the eternal Trinity, this model of authentic feminism pours out her yearning in a prayer of thanksgiving:

> You are a mystery as deep as the sea; the more I search, the more I find, and the more I find the more I search for you. But I can never be satisfied; what I receive will ever leave me desiring more. When you fill my soul I have an even greater hunger, and I grow more famished for your light. I desire above all to see you, the true light, as you really are [in the beatific vision].
>
> I have tasted and seen the depth of your mystery and the beauty of your creation with the light of my under-standing. I have clothed myself with your likeness and have seen what I shall be.[7]

Sadly, the worldly world has not a clue as to what genuine love is all about. This is one reason among dozens of others why a closer look at the saints should be proclaimed over and over from our pulpits and in our presses and electronic media.

LOVE FOR THE CHURCH

The second trait of heroic holiness is a tremendous love for the Church Jesus founded. Because some people have hesitations about this trait, a few introductory observations may be of help.

Loving the Church, which is both "human and divine" (*Sacrosanctum Concilium,* 2), does not mean we love everything some members, past or present, have done or continue to do. Sin, wherever it occurs, is unlovable. However, the first reason we love this Temple of the Holy Spirit (a frequent name given the Church in Vatican Council II) is that Jesus himself loves her and gave himself to death to make her holy (see Ephesians 5:25–26). She must be lovable.

A second reason is that those who follow her teaching and fully embrace her way of life become the splendid men and women we are studying in this book. Sinners become uglier as they reject her teaching or fail to live it; they become less ugly—beautiful even—when they embrace her teaching.

A third reason for our love is that the Church is our mother, who teaches us the path and the means to attain our unspeakable destiny, the beatific vision in risen body. From this Church, which alone goes back to her divine founder, we have the New Testament, the Eucharist, the sacrament of reconciliation and indeed all the sacraments, together with the immensely rich literature that saints and scholars have left us through two thousand years of her history.[8]

Vatican Council II was so convinced of this trait of holiness that it presented love for the Church Jesus founded as a sign of a person's authenticity. In its decree on the training of priests, the council cited a statement of Saint Augustine to the effect that "a man possesses the Holy Spirit to the measure of his love for Christ's Church" (*Optatum Totius,* 9). Strong words indeed.

Jesus himself made a closely connected point when he declared that they who welcome and listen to the ones he sends—that is, the leaders of the infant Church and their successors—welcome and listen to him (see Luke 10:16; John 13:20). This assurance of divine authorization could not be clearer.

Love for the Church necessarily includes love for her magisterial teachings. Saint Thomas More endured imprisonment and a gruesome martyrdom because he gladly supported the papal office and the sanctity of marriage. The twenty centuries of Catholic martyrs, including those in our recent most bloody century, are replete with examples of men and women who died for the truth of divinely revealed doctrines and sound morality. Even though Saint Teresa never became a martyr, she once declared that she was ready to "die a thousand deaths for the faith or for any truth of Sacred Scripture"[9]—a far cry from the attitudes of liturgical and theological dissenters.

We can say that Teresa's consuming love for "His Majesty" was completely mingled with her reasons for reforming Carmel. She intended her monasteries to be supports for the theologians ("learned men," as she called them) who defended the Church and her teachings. She saw her nuns as in love with the Church. So much was this on her mind that, in each of her major works, she goes out of her way to declare her complete submission to the judgment of the Church. A the very outset of *Interior Castle* she declares:

> If I should say something that isn't in conformity with what the holy Roman Catholic Church holds, it will be through ignorance and not through malice. This can be held as certain, and also that through the goodness of God I always am, and will be, and have been subject to her. May He be always blessed and glorified, amen.[10]

As though this were not enough, at the very end of this masterpiece the foundress again assures the reader: "If anything [in this work] is erroneous it is so because I didn't know otherwise; and I submit in everything to what the holy Roman Catholic Church holds, for in this Church I live, declare my faith, and promise to live and die."[11]

We may notice finally that like other saints, when Teresa met failings, even serious ones, in members of the Church, clerical or lay, she never lost her great love for this Temple of the Holy Spirit. What did she do about those faults? She went out and became a saint. As Saint Paul told the Romans, the followers of Jesus overcome evil with good (see Romans 12:14, 17, 21). Teresa overcame evil with heroic goodness.

PROMPT ACTION

Promptness in response to the divine will, however that will is expressed in specific situations, is our next trait of heroic virtue in action. As Saint Ambrose once said in regard to Jesus' mother, the grace of the Holy Sprit knows no delay. In Luke 1:39, when Mary heard that her cousin Elizabeth had conceived a son, she went off to the hill country "as quickly as she could" to be of aid.

That response is typical of the saints. They know nothing of procrastination; they respond to needs as soon as possible. They likewise obey their superiors, whether it be the teaching Church or their local directors, with peaceful immediacy. Teresa wrote at the beginning of *The Interior Castle*:

> Not many things that I have been ordered to do under obedience have been as difficult for me as is this present task of writing about prayer.... But knowing that the

strength given by obedience usually lessens the difficulty of things that seem impossible, I resolved to carry out the task very willingly, even though my human nature seems greatly distressed.[12]

PERFECTION

The fourth trait of lofty virtue is the perfection with which it is practiced. Heroic virtues do not differ in kind from ordinary virtues, but they do differ in the degree of excellence with which they are practiced. Patience, fortitude, temperance or gentleness in a saint is the same quality as in any person, but it is lived in a loftier manner and, as I have noted already, with deeper intensity.

For the saint the motive for being humble or honest or chaste will be more pure of mixed reasons and will spring from a deeper love, the taproot of all the virtues. By pure motivation I refer, of course, to the absence of selfish reasons for performing some good action. When a saint prays in church or chapel, there is no unworthy motive mingled with the desire to adore and love the Lord—that is, there is no concomitant desire to be seen, admired or commended. Another way of putting the matter: the saint is in love—really.

HABITUAL RESPONSE

The practice of heroic virtue is the saint's habitual way of reacting in the situations of daily life. For example, being gentle is the usual manner in which the saintly woman or man deals with the annoyances that are part and parcel of one's state in life. Acts of the virtue are numerous—that is, whenever they are called for in one's concrete circumstances and conditions. Hence, a mother with small children at home and a Poor Clare nun in her cloister are not called to travel in proclaiming the gospel as were Saint Paul and other missionaries.

HEROISM UNDER FIRE

Holy men and women perform heroic actions not only in easy circumstances but also in difficult and profoundly painful ones. The extent of the hardship varies according to circumstances: for example, a child fasting; or a king (Louis, king of France) caring for the sick in a hospital; or a husband and lord chancellor of his country (Thomas More) feeding the poor in his own home; or a drastic degree of factual poverty (Francis of Assisi); or anyone gently welcoming a severe insult or verbal abuse; or a person's devotion to the more perfect course of action in all matters.

INTERCONNECTEDNESS

In her canonization process the Church requires that *all* the virtues be heroic, not simply some of them, and that they be interrelated and influence one another. This trait requires some explanation.

Most people have some qualities but not others: they may be kind but weak or vain; brave but harsh; loyal to one friend but forgetful of or unconcerned about others; chaste but cold; warm but unchaste; precise and faithful but insensitive to others' feelings; outgoing but superficial, gossipy or lazy; efficient and diligent but abrupt with people; generous but selectively so; entertaining but egocentric; altruistic but careless of principles; jovial but dishonest. Since each virtue is an aspect of human goodness, all of them are necessary for completeness: "Be perfect," Jesus said.

This trait of heroic action is a determined giving of everything to the supreme Beloved and to our neighbors for his sake. Psalm 119:10 says it perfectly: "I have sought you with all my heart." The saints, icons of holiness, make a complete break with any tendency to be lukewarm or minimalist. Egocentrism is gone. In the prosaic daily duties of their lives, as well as in the less common spectacular or sensational ones, these women and men are completely faithful.

A Rembrandt painting would not be sublime if some colors clashed with others. Michelangelo's *Pietà* would lack its beauty if some aspects of the Son and his Mother were at odds with others. Sanctity is indeed a most sublime work of art, one beyond our natural powers, a moral miracle.

SEEMINGLY OPPOSITE VIRTUES

Our next trait is the union of seemingly opposite virtues. We must notice carefully the adverb, *seemingly*. There are actually no incompatibilities among gospel gifts, but men and women who lack closeness to God and have little experience or knowledge of the saints may assume that some virtues cannot be reconciled with others and that one may clash with another.

Saints are whole, while the lesser of us tend to be partial. We may have a truth, fasten on it and then forget two or three other truths that condition and qualify it—and keep it sound and sane. Worldly people would take it for granted that a serious contemplative life must clash with a very busy life. But it does not—that is, not in men and women who live the gospel completely, whatever their state in life may be.

For example, Saint Catherine of Siena was an activist in the best sense of the word. Operating on an international level, she was what some called a few years back a "BTO," Big Time Operator. But she was also a mystic, a woman of profoundly deep contemplative intimacy with the Trinity. Saint Francis Xavier likewise was a windmill of activity during the day, but he would immerse himself in profound prayer in the middle of the night.

In giving a goodly number of retreats to married couples over the years, I have found that the most devout of them also live these seeming opposites. And this is only right, for the essentials of the gospel have been proclaimed for everyone in all vocations. Because we know a great deal about Saint Teresa of Avila, and because this Carmelite nun is immensely popular among the faithful, I will with some detail illustrate this trait from her life.

Saint Teresa was a highly gifted woman, both naturally and supernaturally. This nun combined virtues that most people assume without discussion are at odds with one another. Vatican Council II taught us that we all are to be "eager to act and devoted to contemplation" (*Sacrosanctum Concilium*, 2). We should notice the two adjectives, *eager* and *devoted*, not just one or the other. The foundress was exactly so.

Teresa founded no less than eighteen monasteries (establishing one can be a huge task), wrote letters until one or two in the morning and was up with her community for early prayer time. She likewise swept floors in the monastery, wrote books in obedience to her advisors and cared for the ill. Yet she also loved the solitudes of intimacy with the Beloved of her life.

Teresa had a tender love for her family and was not bashful about expressing it, yet at the same time she did not indulge in idle chatter with them, for that would aid them in wasting time, and that is not genuine love. Teresa could be hard-nosed and outspoken in business matters and yet remarkably tender and affectionate in her human relationships. She believed in asceticism and penance, yet she willingly received comfort from others and would say so in her correspondence.

In her many necessary travels founding new monasteries, Teresa and her nuns had healthy fun (not frivolity) and tolerated no gloom along the bumpy roads, while finding ample time for silence and prayer. Teresa had a mind of her own, and she expressed it on occasion, combined with a remarkable spirit of consultation and obedience.

Another popular Carmelite, Saint Thérèse of Lisieux, was likewise striking in her gift of uniting seeming opposites. Human cleverness and strength could not produce so uncommon a gem of femininity, combining warmly expressed affection with a luminous chastity, zealous work with profound contemplative intimacy with God, a robust boldness with genuine humility, strength with tenderness, freedom with discipline. She, too, was God's work of art.

ABIDING JOY

Our final trait of heroism is a thoroughly remarkable joy, even in the midst of severe trials: a joy that this world does not and cannot give. It is also complete and total: this on the word of Jesus himself (see John 15:11). Peter speaks of it in his first letter to the faithful as "a joy so glorious that it cannot be described" (1 Peter 1:8).

Saint Paul admonishes the Philippians to rejoice in the Lord always, not simply when things go well (Philippians 4:4). And he promises the Colossians in all their sufferings, "You will have in you the strength, based on his own glorious power, never to give in, but to bear anything joyfully, thanking the Father" (Colossians 1:11–12).

To get a feel for this remarkable delight, I suggest that you pause for a few moments to consider the most painful day of your life thus far. Perhaps it was a severe verbal abuse from someone you previously respected, an acutely painful illness, an accident that shattered an arm or a leg, a betrayal by your spouse or some other instance of excruciating pain. Now imagine that you bore this pain joyfully—and perhaps you did—and further that you responded by thanking the Father for permitting it. You were likewise aware that this remarkable reaction was due not to your strength, for you had little or none, but to some divinely glorious and received power. You would need no persuasion that this was indeed what we call "a moral miracle."

Now, this is what we find in the saints, and it shines with particular brilliance in the martyr saints. They are men and women full of forgiving love and joy and praise of God as they are being brutally tortured to death. If you have a four-volume set of the *Liturgy of the Hours* or can borrow one from a friend or a library, you can find examples of this joy in suffering in the Office of Readings for the various martyrs.

I note here three excerpts from the lives of such martyrs, because these so perfectly and literally followed their Lord, who was tortured to death for love of us. The first comes from a contemporary writer's account of the crucifixion of the Japanese saints Paul Miki and his companions, during a persecution at the end of the sixteenth century:

> The crosses were set in place.... Brother Martin gave thanks to God's goodness by singing psalms. Again and again he repeated: "Into your hands, Lord, I entrust my

life." Brother Francis Branco also thanked God in a loud voice.... [After thanking God "for this wonderful blessing," Paul Miki continued]: "I do gladly pardon the Emperor and all who have sought my death. I beg them to seek baptism and be Christians themselves." Then he looked at his comrades and began to encourage them in their final struggle. Joy glowed in all their faces.[13]

Our second excerpt, from a letter of the Catholic community of Smyrna, describes the burning at the stake of their holy and highly venerated bishop Polycarp, about the year 155. We take up the account at the moment when all was prepared for the lighting of the fire.

There and then he was surrounded by the material for the pyre. When they tried to fasten him also with nails, he said: "Leave me as I am. The one who gives me strength to endure the fire will also give me strength to stay quite still on the pyre, even without the precaution of your nails.".…

[Saint Polycarp then looked up to heaven and prayed]: "Lord, almighty God,...

I praise you for all things, I bless you, I glorify you through the eternal priest of heaven, Jesus Christ, your beloved Son. Through him be glory to you, together with him and the Holy Spirit, now and for ever. Amen."

When he had said "Amen" and finished the prayer, the officials at the pyre lit it.[14]

Our final illustration comes from a letter of Saint Cyprian, a bishop and himself a martyr, who wrote in the middle of the third century. It is a touching description of what the brutalities of these early executions were like and the splendor with which our ancestors in the faith imitated their Master:

> With what praises can I extol you, most valiant brothers? What words can I find to proclaim and celebrate your brave hearts and your persevering faith? Examined under the fiercest torture, you held out until your ordeal was consummated in glory; it was not you who yielded to the torments but rather the torments that yielded to you....
>
> Tortured men stood there stronger than their torturers; battered and lacerated limbs triumphed over clubs and claws that tore them. *Precious in the sight of God is the death of his holy ones.*"[15]

MORAL MIRACLES: A CLOSER LOOK

To forestall a possible misunderstanding of what I am saying here, let's note what we Catholics understand as a miracle. A miracle is not something unusual or highly unexpected or very difficult to explain, nor simply a tremendous happening in one's life, though some people commonly speak of it as such. A genuine miracle, as we mean it here, is something that cannot happen naturally in our visible universe.

Hence, a physical miracle is an occurrence that cannot be explained by any rigorously demanding and scientifically competent investigation. For example, it is naturally impossible for a person to see without retinas or for certain diseases to be cured instantaneously and permanently. When happenings like these occur at Lourdes, and there is a case for divine intervention, the history of the case and its evidence are carefully studied by a team of physicians. If the case is valid, the cured person must return a year later to give proof of continued health.

Finally the case is sent for confirmation to an international commission in Paris. The bureaus in Lourdes and Paris discern together whether there is any possible natural way to explain the cure, its suddenness, its completeness and its endurance. If not, they send the case to a canonical commission in the diocese of the person cured, and the local bishop decides whether there has or has not been a divine intervention.[16]

A physical miracle, therefore, transcends the powers of nature. A moral miracle is a factual occurrence that transcends the powers and capacities of the human person. It is impossible without divine intervention.

One of the advantages of moral miracles is that they are so attractive and perduring. Another is that many people—that is, those who live with the person so gifted—can experience them personally and directly. A third blessing is that competent and historically accurate written accounts to substantiate the existence of these miracles of heroic virtue are widely available.

Honest men and women know without doubt that they cannot live on the level we have described in this chapter. Nor can they reach by their own powers even a tiny bit of the advanced and transforming contemplative intimacies I presented in the previous chapter. Thus the virtues we see in the saints comprise miracles in the truest sense of the word.

PART III
Consequences

CHAPTER SIX
Scriptural Exegetes

WE BEGIN THIS CHAPTER WITH AN ODD SITUATION. A BIBLICAL exegete is, of course, a professionally trained scholar who has given years, even decades, to the study and analysis of documents composed twenty-some centuries ago. These writings deal with historically verifiable happenings and authentic messages from God. And this God declares that his thoughts and ways are endlessly beyond our merely human thoughts and ways (see Isaiah 55:8–9).

Sensible people would suppose that they need divinely and historically authorized help and guidance in understanding these highly unusual writings. Yet other men and women assume that they know how to explain the Bible—especially their favorite passages. This is the theory of the private interpretation of Scripture, and it is widely held in differing degrees of intensity and often enough in bizarre ways.

But this is not all that is strange. Scholars point out that there are well over twenty thousand different Christian sects in the world; the most recent figure I have come across is twenty-seven thousand. These groups frequently contradict one another in explaining the meaning of particular texts. A basic course in logic will point out that if any one statement flatly and specifically denies what another affirms, one of the two must be wrong—that is, out of touch with reality. For people who are seeking truth, this is no way to proceed.

SAINTS *A Closer Look*

Sacred Scripture itself rules out private interpretation. What Jesus did in founding the Church was to set up a group of apostles who, with their successors, would have authority to teach in his name. So strong and sensible was this plan that he would assure that they understood him rightly in their teaching. The Master was clear: "Anyone who listens to you listens to me; anyone who rejects you rejects me, and those who reject me reject the one who sent me" (Luke 10:16). No wiggle room here.

Jesus clearly established only one Church, which he assured will be right when it teaches with binding authority. To the selected apostles he said, "I tell you solemnly, whatever you bind on earth shall be considered bound in heaven; whatever you loose on earth shall be considered loosed in heaven" (Matthew 18:18). See also Matthew 16:19, where this same remarkable binding authority is given to Peter and his successors when they teach alone. The Lord likewise made it clear that he is with this teaching Church to the very end of time (see Matthew 28:20).

Saint Paul well understood this principle. He said to the Thessalonians: "Another reason why we constantly thank God for you is that as soon as you heard the message that we brought you as God's message, you accepted it for what it really is, God's message and not some human thinking" (1 Thessalonians 2:13).

While private persons may on occasion understand a text of Scripture correctly, they also may be mistaken. History offers thousands of examples, and so does contemporary life.

SAINTS AND SCRIPTURE

Now, how do the saints fit into this picture? Several things need to be noted. First of all, like all the faithful, they are blessed to be subject to the Church's teaching authority—the Magisterium, as we now call it—and to obey it. As I noted in the previous chapter, the saints are happy with this arrangement. The alternative is a welter of private opinions, often contradicting one another.

Second, we have already shown how profoundly the saints are united to their Lord in their transforming intimacy with him. They are therefore privileged possessors of divine light. Once again we notice that the same Holy Spirit who inspired our Scriptures also enlightens those who love much, that they might understand this revelation correctly. Their enlightenment consequently will not be in contradiction to magisterial teaching.

Third, the saints ponder and live the inspired Word thoroughly and thus learn in the very living of what they ponder. Hence their contemplative intimacy, their daily duties and their lightsome understanding all make a beautiful whole. Again, truth is symphonic. This is why Hans Urs von Balthasar could say that the saints are "the great history of the interpretation of the gospel, more genuine and with more power of conviction than all exegesis."[1] Powerful word—and true.

Vatican Council II likewise shed light on the right interpretation of Scripture, both by scholars and by saints. While it is hoped we all appreciate academic competency and expect it in those who speak and write, the council indicated that in the matter of penetrating the meaning of divine revelation, professional skills take second place to saintliness and contemplative intimacy. The reader should notice in the following conciliar citation how its second sentence bristles with the mystical language of advanced communion with God:

> There is a growth in the understanding of the realities and the words which have been handed down. This happens through the contemplation and study made by believers, who treasure these things in their hearts (cf. Luke 2:19, 51), through the intimate understanding of spiritual things they experience. (*Dei Verbum*, 8)

The council here is making three interrelated points: (1) Contemplative intimacy with God takes precedence over personal study if we are to grasp the biblical message authentically and deeply. (2) We must treasure by love these divine realities in order to grow in perceiving their meaning. (3) The experience of "spiritual things" is closely allied with "intimate understanding."

As I have shown, all of this is to happen under and with the guidance of the Church's teaching office. Bishops, priests, theologians, catechists and parents would do well to ponder these words before stepping into a teaching role—whether it be in the classroom, from the pulpit, at home or before a computer.

Fourth, von Balthasar wrote that sin obscures our sight. Realities of the religious, moral and eternal order of things are not clearly perceived by men and women seriously alienated from God by mortal sin, if indeed they are perceived at all. Even venial sins, because they cool love, tend to diminish how well a person perceives these most important of all realities.

Saint Paul was explicit on this point when he told the Corinthians that a worldly person cannot understand divine realities. To such a one divine truth is all "nonsense"; it is simply "beyond his understanding" (1 Corinthians 2:14). It follows that people who readily believe their private interpretations of the Bible are often naïve and too trusting of their own views, which are likely to be colored by the cultures of their times and places.

We can perhaps see better now how and why the Holy Spirit, who has inspired the sacred words of Scripture, also enlightens the saints to understand them in the sense he intended. We are not, of course, implying that the divine inspiration of the Bible is identical with the Spirit's enlightenment of Saints Augustine, Thomas, Catherine, Teresa or the Curé of Ars. Nonetheless, the divine inspirer and enlightener is one Spirit working in unity with the Father and the Son.

Saints explain Scripture in their deeds and in their words. Some are scholars also; many are not. One of the reasons why the Church, both on the local and the universal level, goes through the immense labors and investigations of a single canonization process is that she wants to present what the gospel looks like and means through the attractive examples of heroically holy women and men. They are the master exegetes for adults and children, healthy and ill, poor and rich, ordinary folk and intellectuals, single and married, popes, bishops, priests, consecrated souls—and yes, doctors, lawyers, politicians, judges and businesspeople, too.

Any historically sound biography of a saint illustrates how one man or woman or teenager or child can offer explanations of biblical passages through their ordinary daily activities. I offer here examples of how these saintly ways of living can enrich our own understanding of God's Word and thereby help us live that Word more effectively. It is my hope that these illustrations will alert us to notice these exegetical values when we read about the saints.

RECEIVING DIVINE LIGHT

We are not here dealing with extraordinary phenomena, such as visions or revelations, though God on occasion graces holy ones with such. Rather we are concerned with the ordinary ways in which God enlightens sincere and generous people who strive to center themselves on him.

At the Last Supper Jesus told his apostles that "the Advocate, the Holy Spirit, whom the Father will send in my name, will teach you everything and remind you of all I have said to you" (John 14:26). In the Letter of James we read that "it is all that is good, everything that is perfect, which is given us from above; it comes down from the Father of all light.... By his own choice he made us his children by the message of the truth" (James 1:17–18).

There are many ways in which the Church receives trinitarian light. The first is the pentecostal gift of the Holy Spirit and the magisterial teaching office that Jesus gave to the Church he founded. At the moment we are considering another manner offered to the ordinary faithful and especially to those close to him in an intimate prayer life.

We turn to Saint John of the Cross for help in understanding the two above texts. Experienced as he was with the authentic workings of God in people close to him, he was able to cast light on biblical texts, light not available by mere scholarly methods.

I explained in my book *Fire Within* this saint's lucid teaching about what he terms "locutions."[2] Here I focus on what may be called "assisting enlightenments." When a prayerful person is reflecting on some divine truth (for example, in writing a letter of spiritual direction), he or she often finds that with ease and clarity the mind proceeds to other truths about the matter that had not previously arisen. These new ideas, says John, happen through the aid of the Holy Spirit, who is in every truth.

An assisting enlightenment is not a rare occurrence in sincere people who have a living relationship with the Lord. A prayerful teacher or parent or priest may notice in answering a difficult question that, beginning with some solid truth, new aspects of it or consequences flowing from it occur to his or her mind. At the outset this person "did not know what to say or how to put [the matter], and yet at the moment of composition finds an accompanying enlightenment." Care must be taken, however. "While this assisting locution [literally a 'speaking'] in itself contains no deception, there can be error in the conclusions that the recipient may draw from it."[3]

OVERCOMING EVIL WITH GOOD

As I mentioned earlier, saints "explain" Scripture with their deeds. Take, for example, the scriptural principles on confronting evil.

We meet many painful and depressing problems in our pilgrim journey to final enthrallment. Troubles and trials, major and minor, can seem endless: illnesses, conflicts, arguments, betrayals, liturgical aberrations, rash judgments, misunderstandings, loss of employment, verbal abuse, damaging accidents. Even the helpless innocent are not exempt, as we witness in the brutal extermination of babies in the womb.

The world's way of responding to evil, real or imagined, is retaliation and revenge, bitterness and cynicism, grudge-keeping and name-calling, hatred and terrorism. The Christ-centered way of responding is very different. Jesus on his cross has a revolutionary message. The crucifixion is at once the most ugly of all possible pictures—the horror of torturing infinite innocence to death—and the most beautiful icon of unspeakable love for you and me. Like the Master, we are to overcome evil with good.

Saint Paul puts the principle in three related ways in his Letter to the Romans: "Bless those who persecute you: never curse them, bless them.... Never repay evil with evil.... Resist evil and conquer it with good" (Romans 12:14, 17, 21). Saint Peter is of the same mind: "Never pay back one wrong with another, or an angry word with another one; instead, pay back with a blessing" (1 Peter 3:9).

The saints abound with lived commentaries-in-action on what the crucifix and these apostolic admonitions mean. These are splendid commentaries, powerful and filled with light. Thus we read of Francis kissing a leper, Damien of Molokai becoming a leper among lepers that he might bring the Lord to them, Thérèse smiling at a nun who annoyed her, Teresa of Calcutta and her nuns picking up the dying in the gutters of slums, Robert Bellarmine pawning his cardinal's wall hanging when he needed money to give to a beggar.

When Teresa of Avila experienced laxity in religious life, she went out and founded those eighteen monasteries, with fervent nuns whose love and deep prayer lives would support the Church in troubled days. Francis of Assisi responded to worldliness by covering Europe with his friars, while Dominic,

Ignatius, Angela Merici, John Bosco, Elizabeth Seton and a host of others combated ignorance by gathering dedicated teachers to form schools and other centers of learning.

Camillus de Lellis, Vincent de Paul and many other founders and foundresses established hospitals and religious congregations for the care of the sick, while Elizabeth of Hungary, with her husband's approval, converted one of her castles into a hospital, sold all of her clothing and luxuries to benefit the poor and personally cared for the most repulsively ill. Not surprisingly she was profoundly contemplative.

Not only do these saints offer us splendid commentaries-in-action on overcoming evil with good, but they likewise offer powerful exegesis for other biblical texts. Consider, for example, Jesus' statement that "in so far as you did this to one of the least of these brothers of mine, you did it to me" (Matthew 25:40).

We have in our previous chapter considered the glorious martyrs, who through the centuries loved those who tortured them to death. Our recently completed twentieth century, considered to be the bloodiest in human history, has carried this inspiring testimony of overcoming evil with good into our new millennium.

FRUGALITY: A SHARING LOVE

Both the Old and the New Testaments abound in admonitions about the right use and sharing of material goods. At the same time sincere and religiously minded people—clerical, consecrated and married—who seek to live these gospel ideals have many practical questions, which academic competency alone cannot address adequately. In this matter we again turn to the saints' lived examples, where we find practical answers for each state in life, answers not readily found in textbooks of theology.

So rich is the gospel message on this theme that it takes a book merely to sketch a general picture and then apply it to each vocation. This I attempted to do in *Happy Are You Poor: The Simple Life and Spiritual Freedom* (Ignatius, 2002). Within the confines of this chapter, I will be content to look at a few of the questions that husbands, wives, religious and clerics often raise about their respective states in life. I will offer a few representative biblical texts with some illustrations of how the saints understood, interpreted and applied them in their lives.

Religious-minded married couples currently wonder if they should save for their future retirement, when so many of the destitute in our world have little or nothing to eat. Or they ask if it is right to provide music lessons for their children and to set aside money for their college educations. Clerics and religious ask whether their forsaking of material goods should exceed that of the middle-class laity. Should a convent community have two cars for the sake of convenience or make do with one?

In any state in life there are differing degrees of need. When are things superfluous? To what extent is the provision of frugal beauty in a family home, a monastery, a convent or a rectory compatible with caring for the destitute in Haiti, Calcutta or the slums of one's own city? Is there such a thing as frugal beauty?

First of all, the King of the saints chose to be born not in a royal palace but in a stable. His foster father was an ordinary workman, and both of them engaged in humble labor. During his later travels on foot he chose to have no place to lay his head. He died in complete destitution and with nothing to relieve his agonizing tortures.

Jesus' precursor, Saint John the Baptist, answering the crowd's request as to how they should show genuine conversion, chose among the hundreds of Old Testament precepts the one dealing with a sparing sharing: "If anyone has two tunics he must share with the man who has none, and the one with something to eat must do the same" (Luke 3:11). Matthew reports Jesus' beatitude as "happy are the poor in spirit," while Luke makes it clear that this includes the factually poor (see Matthew 5:3; Luke 6:20).

The Lord also offered some plain and radical comments on social life and parties: "When you give a lunch or a dinner, do not ask your friends, brothers, relations or rich neighbors.... Invite the poor, the crippled, the lame, the blind" (Luke 14:12–13). Saint Thomas More, husband and father, invited the poor into his family home for dinner. Saint Francis of Assisi expected his religious companions to beg their bread, and he wanted them to go without knives to cut it, considering it proper for religious to be content with breaking their loaves with their hands.

Married couples are not usually called to give away their possessions, but all of us should understand the Master's remark, "Where your treasure is, there will your heart be also" (Luke 12:34). Saint Peter declared the deepest feminine beauty to consist not in the artificiality of external garb and jewelry but in the inner splendor of holiness (see 1 Peter 3:3–5).

Loving God totally, the saints see material goods as aids to sharing that love with needy sisters and brothers. So it was with Saint Robert Bellarmine, who would take his hat off to the beggar at the door and invite him to be seated on the same chair that visiting cardinals used. Robert gave not only money but also respect and love, a lived bit of exegesis we all need.

CONTEMPLATIVE INTIMACY WITH GOD

Another area in which saintly lived exegesis outstrips the capacities and limits of mere academic scholarship is that of biblical texts dealing with contemplative prayer. The psalmist's "one thing," his top priority in life, his overriding necessity, is to "dwell in the house of the LORD" and "to behold the beauty of the LORD" (Psalm 27:4, *RSV*). He invites us to "look to [God], and be radiant" and "taste and see that the LORD is good" (Psalm 34:5, 8, *RSV*). The prayerful person thirsts for his God "as in a dry and weary land" (Psalm 63:1, *RSV*).

This brings to mind again Saint Paul's remarkably strong statement of our being "filled with the utter fulness of God" (Ephesians 3:19). I explained in chapter four how well Saints John of the Cross and Teresa of Avila described the sublime depths of these interpersonal intimacies in their works and lived them in their contemplative immersion in the Trinity. Unless biblical scholars and theologians are aware of these same profound experiences, they simply cannot explain what the inspired Word means in passages like these.

It is not only John and Teresa who are excellent exegetes of this "one thing," the summit of human relationships with the divine on earth. We can add men and women like Bernard of Clairvaux, Catherine of Siena and—much earlier, in the fifth century—John Chrysostom. By a happy choice the *Liturgy of the Hours* includes a homily of the last named patristic giant dealing with the deepest intimacies with Triune Beauty. A few brief excerpts explain our biblical texts in a manner far beyond academic expertise.

John Chrysostom tells his congregation that this unifying and profound communion with God is the highest good, the *summum bonum*. He is careful to point out that he is not speaking of routine recitations nor of mere words uttered at set times. Rather he is talking about a deep intimacy that is "continuous throughout the day and night"—which sounds like the transforming union being taught to all the faithful, which indeed it should be.

This remarkable bishop goes on to say that this advanced prayer is given by the Lord (*infused* is our word today) and includes "inexpressible longings," quoting Saint Paul (Romans 8:26). He says: "One who tastes this food is set on fire.... His spirit burns as in a fire of the utmost intensity." Here we have a pastor dealing with what all bishops and priests should be proclaiming from their pulpits, a splendid commentary on our biblical texts.[4]

Biblical scholar Father Barnabas Ahern once noted that he wished that he understood the New Testament as well as Saint Thérèse of Lisieux did. Books and articles about Thérèse abound. Critical editions of her writings and letters and the recorded conversations she had during her final illness are all eloquent testimonies to the thesis we are developing in this chapter. So too are the multitudes of men and women in all states of life and throughout the world who have been deeply touched by her person and her thoughts.

Thérèse is especially known for her living and teaching about the childlike trust and "littleness" of which Jesus himself spoke: "Unless you change and become like little children you will never enter the kingdom of heaven. And so, the one who makes himself as little as this little child is the greatest in the kingdom of heaven" (Matthew 18:3–4). How do mature and responsible adults live like children? Why and how are the two ideals of maturity and childlikeness not only compatible but also desirable?

I cannot imagine a mere scholar answering these questions with the ease, accuracy and charm that flowed so spontaneously from a very young woman who had no college degree. Thérèse offers us lived and verbal responses to these and other questions, not only in the small, routine details of daily life but even in the stark physical pains and darkness of her final months. Her heroic life remains a splendid commentary not only on this text but on others as well, such as the greatest of all commandments: How does one *be* love in the Church? Thérèse's life and death are splendid commentaries on this question for every one of us.

EXEGETICAL GEMS IN BRIEF

Since there is no visible end to the possible illustrations of saintly exegesis, we will content ourselves now with several concisely mentioned examples. The prophet Baruch advises us on how to repent of our sins: "As by your will you first strayed away from God, so now turn back and search for him ten times as hard" (4:28). But we wonder, how do we repent and search for the Lord ten times harder than we have strayed from him? I think immediately of Saint Augustine's classic masterpiece *Confessions,* which magnificently answers dozens of aspects of holy, love-filled, completely trusting sorrow and healing.

For a shorter commentary we can ponder the example of Saint Mary Magdalene's loving, trusting repentance in the Gospels, an instance of the Bible explaining the Bible. We learn what mere scholarship could not teach: how to have complete confidence in divine mercy and a burning love penetrating that confidence as well as our sorrow. We learn that no matter what our past may be, we too are called to the heights of union with the Trinity, who is endless love.

Few people seem impressed with certain aspects of Jesus' teaching. Take for example his statement that we shall give an account on judgment day "for every unfounded word" we utter (Matthew 12:36). Commonly no problem is seen in excessive chatter. Yet we are told in the wisdom literature that "a flood of words is never without its fault" (Proverbs 10:19). An exaggeration? What possibly could be wrong with a mere excess of words?

Fifteen or twenty examples could be mentioned. Not wanting to be guilty of an excess of words myself, let me note a few that immediately come to mind: detraction, calumny, exaggeration, egocentrism, waste of time, neglect of work and of prayer. Saint Teresa in her later life expressed regret a number of times for her earlier excesses in speech. We also read that Saint Dominic "seldom spoke unless it was with God, that is, in prayer, or about God."[5] Saints see what lesser folk tend not even to notice.

One of the most difficult questions sincere people ask is whether and when and how they are to fulfill the obligation to correct others: husband, wife, relative, friend, neighbor, parishioner, fellow worker, yes, even one's superior. Jesus is clear about the need for fraternal admonition: "If your brother does something wrong, go and have it out with him alone, between your two selves" (Matthew 18:15). We should notice that the first step in a situation of significant fault is not to gossip about it with a third party or to report the matter to the superior. The Lord insists that instead we go to the person involved—and with gentleness, honesty and love.

Saint Paul plainly states that we are to "teach each other, and advise each other, in all wisdom" (Colossians 3:16). Again there are no age or status restrictions. The book of Proverbs several times declares that we should welcome being corrected by others. For example, "Rebuke a wicked man, you get insult in return....Rebuke a wise man and he will love you for it....He grows wiser still" (9:7–9). It goes without saying that heroically humble men and women welcome being admonished, and this is one of the reasons why they heal so rapidly of their faults.

Saints Bernard and Catherine stand out in history as models of when and how to admonish others, bishops and religious superiors included. As Paul did regarding Peter, they went to the person involved, not to third parties. They were informed, honest and completely obedient to their superiors. Most of all they were burning with love, a trait rare in critical, complaining people. If today's critics possessed these traits, they would enjoy a great deal more credibility.

Saint Paul demonstrated his warm love for the community he corrected and for the particular wrongdoer:

> When I wrote to you, in deep distress and anguish of mind, and in tears, it was not to make you feel hurt but to let you know how much love I have for you.

...The punishment already imposed by the majority on the man in question is enough; and the best thing now is to give him your forgiveness and encouragement, or he might break down from so much misery. (2 Corinthians 2:4, 6–7)

A fine piece of exegesis in action.

Then there are the questions that can become notable problems for generous people: To what extent should we sacrifice and give ourselves for the welfare of others, especially those outside the immediate family? Are there limits? If so, where does one draw the line?

What academic can answer these questions wisely? It is not likely that biblical scholars will attempt to spell out details as to how we should respond in our unique situations. The saints give us lived guides, Spirit-inspired pointers as to what gladly spending and being spent for others looks like.

I think immediately of the apostles after Pentecost, Paul, Francis Xavier, Junípero Serra, Isaac Jogues and John de Brebeuf. Then there are the teaching and nursing religious women and men who exhausted themselves for the sake of children, the sick and the elderly. The Curé of Ars and Padre Pio suffered the white martyrdom of hours on end in the labors of the confessional. Each of these heroically zealous ones is a living exegesis of the total self-giving we find in the New Testament and the love that motivates it.

PERFECT PERSPECTIVE

Our next illustration of lived exegesis deals with the trait of revelation that is pervasive throughout Scripture. I refer to perspective and proportion: seeing big things as big, small things as small—an extremely hard thing to do unless one is a saint or getting close to being one. God's Word envisions and presents the wide picture, the overridingly important realities.

What are some of these realities of supreme importance? Our Triune God, the Incarnation, the Eucharist, the Church Jesus founded and loves, the theological and moral virtues, our destiny in eternity, a deep prayer life.

Now, unless one is well on the road to holiness, it is very difficult in the midst of a daily routine to see things in perspective, as they really are. In a disagreement between spouses, for example, the large matter is that they be gentle and show love for each other in word, action, manner and tone of voice. What are small are their petty preferences: "my way, what I like and want, what is convenient for me." Especially when anger is involved, the little things take on a false importance, while the essential matter of love is completely forgotten. I find it refreshing that saints see thing exactly as they are, neither more nor less. Saint Paul himself presents a striking example in his Second Letter to the Corinthians. In chapter eleven we find an imposing list of the brutal sufferings and seemingly endless hardships he met in his labors on behalf of his people, whom he loved dearly: harsh imprisonments; repeated bloody beatings of various types (lashes, sticks, stoning), often to the point of death; dangers from rivers and at sea, from robbers, pagans and even his own people. He knew hunger and thirst, cold and sleepless nights; and finally there were his worries and his concern for the communities he had founded.

While most people would consider one of these sufferings notable, if not huge, Paul looked at all of them as of little account—that is, as both short in duration when compared to eternity and small in their brutality when seen realistically as preparing him for the unspeakable "weight of eternal glory which is out of all proportion to them" (2 Corinthians 4:17). On both counts he is exactly right: perfect perspective and proportion.

I cannot imagine anyone but a saint seeing the significance of bitter suffering for the gospel with such crystal clarity. We lesser ones, in our daily Masses and *Liturgy of the Hours* (both made up mostly from the Scriptures), have continual reminders of this perspective, and yet we are slow to acquire this vision of reality. Only heroic virtues and contemplative union with Triune Light bring it about.

THE EXEGETICAL QUINTESSENCE

This brings us to our final example of the saints as living commentaries on how to concretize God's Word in our lives. I refer to the greatest of all virtues: love, total love. How do we live complete, selfless love in our own state of life?

To answer this question we choose three closely related New Testament examples, which together describe the core of being a saint. The first is a purifying requirement: "What we have to do is to give up everything that does not lead to God" (Titus 2:12). We return to Saint Paul's positive proclamation of this mandate, "Whatever you eat, whatever you drink, whatever you do at all, do it for the glory of God" (1 Corinthians 10:31).

These two texts, when lived totally, bring about a revolutionary conclusion: "To love is to live according to his commandments,...to live a life of love" (2 John 1:6). Only God could originate so exquisite an idea in six short syllables: to live a life of love! But one will wonder, what in the world does this mean?

It is difficult to imagine a more insightful and more moving commentary on these words than Saint John of the Cross provides. His own experience gave rise to his descriptions of a human person so intimately one with the indwelling Father, Son and Holy Spirit that he or she has become "all love." To get something of a taste for this saint's experience and its exegetical light, I borrow a paragraph from *Fire Within:*

> In the transforming union the person is now "all love," and all her actions are love. By this John means that love is not restricted simply to formal times of prayer and to ejaculations scattered through the day. Rather everything—seeing, hearing, tasting, working, resting, playing—triggers love in and through all things. This person is quite literally fulfilling the greatest of all the commandments: she [he] is loving God with her whole heart, soul and mind. "The soul easily extracts the sweetness of love from all the things that happen to her; that is, she loves God in them. Thus everything leads her to love." Whether her daily experiences are delightful or bitter, she finds the Beloved in them and "knows nothing else but love" for Him in each of them.[6]

This is biblical exegesis at its best: authentic, clear, accurate, brilliant, moving. It comes from the mind, heart and experience of a very great saint.

CONCLUSIONS

Among the many consequences that we may draw from our reflections in this chapter, I may suggest four that stand out.

First of all, note that the saints are Catholic. This refers not only to their belonging to our ecclesial community and partaking in the wholeness of the one revelation of Jesus Christ but also to their living in many nations and cultures and centuries. (Recall that *catholic* means "universal.") Knowing them well expands our minds and assumptions beyond the limitations, narrowness and biases of our own country, culture and customs.

One of the side benefits of my own vagabonding for the Lord, at home and abroad over several decades, is a freedom from similar limitations, yielding a wider outlook on reality. I have seen firsthand how our one Catholic truth is lived in many different lands and places. The saints over the whole world and through the centuries do this for all of us on a grander scale.

Our second conclusion follows from the first. Jesuit Father Raymond Gawronski put it well: "The saints are the concrete norms, the ongoing exegesis of Christ throughout time."[7] Mother Church presents her divinely secured truth not only in abstract doctrinal and moral formulas (important as these are for accuracy and clarity) but also in the visible icons that her heroes and heroines of holiness actually are. And these are what they are precisely because they embrace and live so well this mother's teaching and partake in her sacraments with such fervor.

Third, by knowing the saints well, we gradually grow in thinking as they think and in judging and choosing as they judge and choose. Thus we share more fully in the light they receive "from the Father of all light" (James 1:17). Seeing reality more realistically provides us with ready solutions to many of our daily questions and problems that are not raised in books and lectures.

For example, how do I deal with *this* annoying person? How do I practically solve my time-pressure problem? How do I use and share material goods in my state of life and in my circumstances? When is my use of television, radio and Internet actually for the glory of God and my own genuine good, and when is it not? When do I really eat and drink for this same glory, and when do I not?

The Church explicitly exhorts us in her liturgies to look to the saints for light, which they reflect from the Son, who is "the light of the world" (John 8:12), in a manner similar to the moon's reflection of the light of the sun. On the Feast of Saint Bernard, the liturgy puts on our lips an address to the saint himself: "Blessed Bernard, your life, flooded by the splendor of the divine Word, illumines the Church with the light of true faith and doctrine."[8] On the Feast of Saint Teresa of Avila we pray that we may be "fed with her heavenly teaching."[9]

Finally, when we celebrate the Feast of John of the Cross, we are urged "to imitate him always."[10] This reminds me of Pope Pius XI's comment that John's teaching is pure gospel.

CHAPTER SEVEN
Marvelous Teachers

WHILE IT IS TRUE THAT THE SAINTS ARE TEACHERS BECAUSE they are outstanding exegetes, both in action and in word, in this chapter we envision two other facets of their enlightening gifts to God's people. Whether they are scholars or not, we now consider them as communicators of the divine message via spoken and written words. Then we will explain in what ways they should be considered theological sources.

We begin with the theological giants, those light-filled men so close to the incarnate Word not only chronologically—by living in the first centuries of the Christian dispensation—but also in spirit, truth and love. Of them Hans Urs von Balthasar has written:

> Greatness, depth, boldness, flexibility, certainty and a flaming love—the virtues of youth, are marks of patristic theology. Perhaps the Church will never again see the likes of such an array of larger-than-life figures such as mark the period from Irenaeus to Athanasius, Basil, Cyril, Chrysostom, Ambrose and Augustine—not to mention the army of the lesser Fathers. Life and doctrine are immediately one. Of them all is true what Kierkegaard said of Chrysostom: "He gesticulated with his whole existence."[1]

Yes, these men gesticulated not only with their words of intellectual brilliance but also with their vibrant zeal, love and prayer. Of them the Master spoke with a special pertinence when he declared in the Sermon on the Mount, "You are the light of the world" (Matthew 5:14). No other religion has teachers like these.

SAINT AUGUSTINE

A look at Augustine shows us a man who wrote, spoke and prayed—yes, "gesticulated"—with his whole being. In his masterpiece *The Trinity*, he manifests an astonishing recall and understanding of Scripture, both the Old and the New Testaments. This grasp concerned myriads of texts and their likely or sure meanings, together with their interrelationships. Saint Robert Bellarmine centuries later had a similar recall ability, citing up to 150 pertinent patristic texts in support of a theological point he was writing about.

Shining forth also in Augustine's scholarship is his wonder at the splendor and beauty of divine revelation and of the Lord of it all. Even on the natural level, a teacher who imparts information but does not excite wonder in students is only half a teacher. A biology instructor who does not marvel with his listeners as he explains the vastly intricate manufacturing plant, transportation system and computer-like technology in each of the trillions of cells in the human body is lacking in his career. When we listen to a speaker who mingles intellectual brilliance with marveling at what he is communicating, we see what the prophet Daniel meant in saying that teachers of holiness shall shine like "stars for all eternity" (Daniel 12:3).

The bishop of Hippo shows us also in his literary labors, most likely unwittingly, how our work is to be integrated with our contemplative intimacy with God. This commingling made his classic *Confessions* a new literary form: a long, book-length prayer, a work that is itself a shared and moving communion with God.

This unified blending of action and contemplation is found also in *The Trinity*. Even as Augustine labored mightily through its many pages, he was seeking to know the three divine Persons more perfectly and to love them more ardently. This burning pursuit of Triune Beauty was the focus of his being and of his scholarly work.

Likewise obvious in his literary labors is a love for his readers and others—learned and unlearned alike—who would hear or read his words. He did not forget that he was a bishop instructing and feeding the flock committed to his care by Jesus himself. These he sought to enlighten and to lead on to a still deeper love of and service to Father, Son and Holy Spirit. Some members of his audience well may have wept to experience the warm love of their pastor for them and his concern for their eternal welfare.

From the vast literary legacy of Augustine we select two of his lesser-known gems as illustrations of his gesticulating by life and by word. Addressing his much-loved Lord, the saint declared, "Anyone who loves something else along with you, but does not love it for your sake, loves you less."[2] Behind this statement lies a wealth of theological truths dealing with creation as reflecting and flowing from the divine *fiat*—with our human orientation to the infinite God and to nothing less; with the totality of genuine love; with the consequent exclusion of idols, major or minor; with the universal call to deep conversion, all the way to the elimination of venial sins and even on to heroic virtue, and with our call to the summit of intimacy with Father, Son and Holy Spirit.

Our second gem is a mere seven words—indeed, in English translations, seven syllables: "To pray well, one must live well."[3] A deepening intimacy with the Trinity is life, the supreme life. Living things are meant to grow to full maturity. A rosebush should not merely sprout out of the ground; it should produce radiant blooms. To pray well here means to grow in meditative communion and then to proceed on to receive (when ready for it) contemplative depth from God. This happens when we experience the depths of conversion.[4] The master teacher and pastor said all of this in seven syllables.

OTHER MASTER TEACHERS

Saint Thomas Aquinas is another example of what we have in mind. His philosophical and theological insights have been pondered, mined, explored and taught from the thirteenth century to the present day, and there are no signs of these studies ceasing. A tiny taste of what we have in mind here was offered by Thomistic scholar Etienne Gilson when he commented on Chesterton's unique and delightful biography of the angelic doctor: "Chesterton makes one despair. I have been studying St. Thomas all my life and I could never have written such a book. I consider it as being without possible comparison the best book ever written on St. Thomas. Nothing short of genius can account for such an achievement."[5] Indeed, it is no exaggeration to say that reading Gilson on Thomas is a rare treat.

I have already spoken at some length about Saints Teresa of Avila and John of the Cross. Historian Christopher Dawson has two sentences concerning these two Carmelites that make our point in a striking manner. The first provides the context, the second the message:

To me at least the art of the Counter Reformation was a pure joy, and I loved the churches of Bernini and Borromini no less than the ancient basilicas. And this in turn led me to the literature of the Counter Reformation, and I came to know St. Teresa and St. John of the Cross, compared to whom even the greatest non-Catholic religious writers seem pale and unreal.[6]

That a woman several centuries ago who never, as far as I can tell, sat in a school classroom would become one of the most widely read of Spanish writers is quite unheard of. That she was highly intelligent we know, but the realism to which Dawson refers was due to grace, to the fact that this woman had met the living God most intimately and authentically in her profound prayer life and to her unforgettable experiences of him.

Basically the same must be said of Saint John of the Cross. Literary experts consider him among the very best of Spanish poets, and he is so utterly real because he knew firsthand what he was writing about. Yes, both he and Teresa had learned much from sacred Scripture and the teaching Church, but they also personally experienced what they taught so effectively. Of them we can say with von Balthasar:

Those who above all have undergone and enjoyed such experiences [of God] have in every age been the saints. Church history is above all, perhaps, the history of the saints, known and unknown. Those who have staked everything on one card, and by their daring have become pure mirrors, have in a rich spectrum cast the light from within on to our dark outside. They are the great history of the interpretation of the gospel, more genuine and with more power of conviction than all exegesis. They are the proof both of the fulness and of the presence.[7]

This is why their works have all the marks of authenticity and attraction for the sincere and God-seeking men and women of our own day.

One could go on and on with other master teachers among the heroic ones: Catherine of Siena, Thérèse of Lisieux, Francis de Sales and a large number of others, but this volume is only an introduction. It will achieve one of its purposes if readers go on to read the lives and writings of these men and women.

THEOLOGICAL SOURCES

I want to be careful to rule out misunderstandings of the above subhead. Though some of the saints have received authentic private revelations, in the Catholic Church we base our theology on the solid and sure public communications God has given through the prophets of the Old Testament and, most of all, through Jesus and his apostles in the new dispensation. Hence we are not here referring to private communications that the Lord at times shares with those intimate with him. Likewise we are not suggesting that ordinary saints are originating sources of divine insights, such as we have in the biblically inspired Scriptures. Nor, finally, are we intimating that all saints are intellectuals in our contemporary sense of the term; some are and some are not.

What I do mean here by "theological sources" is that saints do what theology books, catechetical outlines and lectures cannot adequately do. These holy ones embody the revealed message—that is, public revelation historically verifiable— with particular examples and applications for all states in life.

Their lives and words explain for each of us how God's Word is to be understood and applied in "my situation, my particular circumstances, which are often different from yours."

Another aspect of these "theological sources" is to note that Jesus, radiant image of the Father's glory (see Hebrews 1:1–3), cannot be fully portrayed to the world by any one saint. But all of them together, with their many gifts and charisms, come closer to this ideal. So when we see them, we are helped to know both Jesus and his Father better. For they who see the Son see the Father as well (see John 14:7–13).

Saints are, of course, theological sources for the reasons we consider them scriptural exegetes, as I explained in the previous chapter. Being led to heroic virtues by the same Holy Spirit who has inspired sacred Scripture, they become superior pictures of what his divine Spirit had in mind when he inspired the Bible. Truth is symphonic. It makes one beautiful whole because it has one divine source.

There is still one final facet to this picture. Because love sees in special ways (see 1 John 4:7–8), and because saints burn with love for the supreme Light, they enjoy a privileged access to the divine intent. They readily see through the falsehoods of dissenting theology—which is why there are no cafeteria spiritualities among the saints. To them it is obvious that rejecting the proclamation of those whom Jesus sent in his name and with his authority is a distortion of supernatural reality and a rejection of God himself (see Luke 10:16).

With a heavenly instinct they also grasp why the specialties in theological studies (biblical, doctrinal, moral, ascetical, contemplative) should be integrated. Saints have, for example, a privileged understanding of heroic virtues because they know them experientially and not merely in abstract theological formulations. Living a life of love themselves, they possess a living understanding of what the supernatural economy of salvation is all about and how everything fits together. Once again, the saints are God's favored work of art.

ACADEMIC HONESTY

I return here to the issue of academic honesty, mentioned among the basic attitudes of saints in chapter three. I need to point out that responsible rigor is not the practice of all scholars.

My three chief academic interests over the years have been Scripture, theology and science. Reading and study in these fields has suggested a number of remarkable convergences between Scripture rightly interpreted and what our best scientists have to say.[8] But I also have noticed repeated differences between theologians and some scientists. The differences are between candor and cover-up—that is, between facing objections and problems openly and not facing or even mentioning them.

Augustine, Thomas and their colleagues would not have dreamed of covering up or declining to respond to difficulties. They took it for granted that such would be dishonest and therefore displeasing to God. But I notice scientists who, in writing textbooks and articles aimed at the general public, bypass solid scientific evidence and do not even attempt to respond to objections to their positions. An example will illustrate this lack of academic virtue.

I have no theological problem with the idea of evolution: God can use secondary causes in his creation whenever he wishes. But microbiologists, with whom I fully agree, have huge problems with random-chance theories of natural selection.

One objection is that the fantastic complexities of living cells were already present at the very beginnings of bacterial life—with no hint of slow, incremental developments and no scientific evidence as to how they came to be. Israeli physicist Gerald Schroeder notes in *The Hidden Face of God: Science Reveals the Ultimate Truth:*

> [Elso Barghoorn of Harvard] searched the surfaces of polished slabs of stone taken from the oldest of rocks able to bear fossils. To the amazement of the scientific community, fossils of fully developed bacteria were found in rocks 3.6 billion years old.... Overnight, the fantasy of billions of years of random reactions in warm little ponds brimming with fecund chemicals leading to life, evaporated. Elso Barghoorn had discovered a most perplexing fact: life, the most complexly organized system of atoms known in the universe, popped into being in the blink of a geological eye.[9]

I can respect Charles Darwin for stating that if the geological strata were later to fail to disclose evidence for many gradual and transitional forms of species, his theories would collapse. We now know that such is the case. Biologist Lewis Thomas has pointed out that what the strata do show is that every new species to appear in the fossil records is perfect according to its kind. I have found no admission of this huge objection in any disciple of Darwin.

In November 2004 *National Geographic* carried a lengthy article titled "Was Darwin Wrong?"[10] The answer, of course, was negative, and yet there was no mention of this towering objection, nor was there admission of numerous other cogent objections stemming from microbiology.[11] To be fair to the periodical, I should mention that in a later issue there appeared a letter to the editor that nicely summarized my thought here in one sentence: "You do not address any of the gaping holes in the theory that lead so many reasoned people to question evolution."[12]

Scholarly saints leave no gaping holes. They love truth, the whole truth. Saint Augustine, who manifests an unquestioning adherence to the inspired Word, a profound love for truth, a marvelous humility and an unlimited love for the Triune Beauty, is not afraid of contrary viewpoints, as his prologue to book 3, chapter 1 of *The Trinity* shows:

> What I desire for all my works, of course, is not merely a kind reader but also a frank critic. This is peculiarly my desire for this work, treating as it does of so tremendous a subject, in which one wishes as many discoverers of truth could be found as it certainly has contradictors. But the last thing I want is a reader who is my doting partisan, or a critic who is his own. The reader will not, I trust, be fonder of me than of Catholic faith, nor the critic of himself than of Catholic truth. To the first I say: "Do not show my works the same deference as the canonical scriptures. Whatever you find in scripture that you used not to believe, why, believe it instantly. But whatever you find in my works that you did not hitherto regard as certain, then unless I have really convinced you that it is certain, continue to have your doubts about it." To the second I say: "Do not criticize what I write by the standard of your own prejudices or contrariness, but by the divine text or incontrovertible reason."[13]

In chapter five I quoted from the prayer with which Augustine ended this work. His humble conclusion to that prayer is "O Lord the one God, God the Trinity, whatsoever I have said in these books is of you, may those that are yours acknowledge; whatsoever of myself alone, do you and yours forgive. Amen."[14]

This is kneeling theology at its best. Would that in our day we had more imitators, among theologians and other academics as well. If more had this love for truth combined with this humility, we would be spared not a few painful problems.

Let us thank and honor God for the holy teachers he has given us. Surely they deserve our gratitude. And surely God will reward them for their pursuit of truth and their courage in presenting it. "The learned will shine brightly as the vault of heaven, and those who have instructed many in virtue, as bright as stars for all eternity" (Daniel 12:3).

CHAPTER EIGHT
Freedom

FOR MOST WORLDLY MINDED PEOPLE, THE TITLE OF THIS CHAPTER would be among the last ideas they would connect with saintliness. To them it is sinners—who do whatever they have a mind or inclination to do—who enjoy freedom. But men and women who are more or less given to this assumption quite surely have spent little time thinking seriously about the matter.

While it is true that all through human history our ancestors have misused words, usually unintentionally, in our age of the mass media the problem has become rampant and acute. Strong, powerful terms have been weakened and distorted through carelessness, overuse and a proclivity to exaggeration. *Love,* for example, in its genuine gospel meaning, is a generous, self-sacrificing giving to another, even if little or nothing is received in return. Yet today the word is often used as a cover-up for lust, the egocentric exploitation of another person.

Pro-choice is a euphemism used to justify the brutal extermination of a baby in the mother's womb. They who distort this word seem not to realize that every sin is pro-choice: rape, robbery, lying, gossip, murder are all pro-choice and pro-selfishness. Too bad about the victim.

If a pollster were to ask fifty people in downtown New York or London or Paris, "What do you think freedom is?" most by far would answer something like, "Having fewer laws and rules," or, "Being able to do what you want to do with nobody interfering." There is a kernel of truth in these responses, but they miss the very core of human liberty.

FREE TO DO AND THUS TO BE

We cannot understand the freedom of the saints (or our own freedom for that matter) until we grasp what freedom actually is. Freedom and choice are strong, precious gifts that raise the human person above other creatures in the visible universe. At its root our freedom is the self-determining power to do and thus to be. A few examples make this clear.

The main reason I am not free to play a piano is not that there is some law holding me back. My problem is that I do not have the needed knowledge and skills, the power, to play this instrument. So also I am free to use a computer only if I have an intellect and a will, together with a bit of computer know-how.

Teachers are free to teach accounting or biology or theology only if they know their subjects and have the communication skills needed to convey their knowledge to students. A surgeon is free to do a triple bypass and a cook to prepare a meal only to the extent that they are competent.

Thus, at the root of freedom are knowledge and skills. A consequence of having these powers is that the person should not be unreasonably impeded from using them. But without the basic power to do or not to do, there can be no question of freedom.

Furthermore, we should remember the plain lesson of experience that sin by its nature enslaves and degrades a person (see John 8:34; 2 Peter 2:19). This is completely obvious in cases of addiction: drugs, alcohol, lust, overeating. But even lesser sins tend toward differing degrees of debasement: grouchiness, rage, vanities, snapping at others, being tied to hours of television or the Internet. Habits of these types diminish our worth, deaden our personalities and lessen our potential for goodness, genuine beauty and joy.

Saints are empowered by truth and goodness to be liberated from all sorts of possible human ugliness. They become honest, loving, humble, pure, altruistic, patient, strong. This is why they have little need for rules and laws (see 1 Timothy 1:9). Being prompted and led by the Holy Spirit, they enjoy the glorious freedom of goodness. In the splendid statement of Saint Paul, the Spirit has transformed them from one glory, one beauty, to another, even into the divine image (see 2 Corinthians 3:17–18).

In a nutshell, therefore, this liberation of the sons and daughters of God is a freedom of goodness. Twenty centuries ago Jesus made this truth as clear as the noonday sun—if only we would pay attention: "If you make my word your home you will indeed be my disciples, you will learn the truth and the truth will make you free" (John 8:31–32). To possess truth is to be in touch with reality, the way things really are, and it is reality, not our imaginary fantasies, that makes us beautiful.

It follows that there are degrees of personal freedom. We become more or less free to do anything to the degree that we possess an ability or capacity: to play basketball, sing a song, teach a class; to be patient, chaste, loving, temperate. Just as there are degrees of conversion and intimacy with the indwelling Trinity in prayer, so there are degrees of being able to act and to be on higher and higher levels.

REMAINING FREE

We can see how the gospel concept of freedom (which is also plain common sense) vastly surpasses the worldly ideas of "Don't hem me in," and "Let me do just as I please," which actually mean, "Let me debase myself," "Let me become unlovely," "Let me become morally ugly," "Let me become a slave."

Clinging to created things for their own sake—attachment—may look to the hedonist and the irreligious like liberation for a life of unlimited pleasure-seeking. Actually, however, it is a gradual sinking into a deepening bondage, into a state of being less and less capable of experiencing the grand delights of personal fulfillment. It forsakes the search for intimacy with Triune Beauty, which Paul, Augustine, Bernard, Catherine, Teresa and John can only describe as indescribable. To miss this is to miss everything.

We can look at genuine freedom in still another way: that is, by taking a closer look at selfish attachments. A simple definition will help. An attachment in the pejorative sense of the term is a clinging of the will to something created for its own sake. It is a kind of idol worship: either a major idol—a mortal sin of avarice, arrogance or lust, for example—or a minor idol such as a petty vanity, overeating, laziness, useless television or Internet.

I am not referring here to the legitimate pleasure we can experience in something good and worthwhile—though there is a danger of pursuing any pleasure to excess or for its own sake. We can possess and use things without being attached to them: God made creation good in order that it would lead us to him. Nor is being attracted to someone or something an attachment—though again there is the danger of making the beautiful person or thing an idol, sought for its own sake and to the exclusion of the one God.

One may ask at this point, "When are desires disordered and thus leading to bondage?" There are three signs:

- One is that the thing sought is diverted from its purpose. For example, using speech to lie or gossip or engage in idle chatter, with all its dangers of detraction, calumny, egocentrism and lazy neglect of duties.

- A second sign is excess: eating and drinking too much or spending too much time in mere amusements.

- A third sign is making means into ends—that is, using things for their own sakes and not for bringing ourselves and others closer to God and our final destiny. These twistings of reality entail a gradual sinking into a lessening of freedom and even at times into addictions.

Centering on created things for themselves lessens our capacity to say no and thus diminishes freedom. Psychic energy and freedom are dissipated as self-indulgence increases.

Saints have no enslaving idols, major or minor. Which is to say that they have no disordered desires. Their only god is God, and they are free to grow into being more and more what we are all called to be: fully God's works of art.

Saint Paul suggests this when he says that having nothing, he has everything (see 2 Corinthians 6:10). He is a completely fulfilled person because he is open to love. He can embrace without hindrances what *"no eye has seen and no ear has heard,"* indeed what we cannot even imagine (1 Corinthians 2:9). In the highest degrees of heroic virtue, the saint is free to live "a life of love" (2 John 1:6), which is a life of growing more beautiful in all of the large and small details of daily life.

CHAPTER NINE
Spiritualities

IF I WERE ASKED TO NAME THE CHIEF OBSTACLES SERIOUS PEOPLE face today in their pursuit of God, my list would be topped by secularism, sensuality and pseudo "spiritualities." We may assume here that most of our readers are well aware of the first two problems; in this chapter we shall be concerned with the last named.

It is safe to say that religious bookstores are bursting with popular but shallow books that claim to address our human need for something transcending the material universe. The unwary can be misled by an abundance of superficial and unfounded "spiritualities," which are likewise propagated in magazines and on television and the Internet. Television and the Internet similarly are saturated with both subtle and blatant appeals to the millions who are pursuing the "transcendent more" where it cannot be found. Deep down even the playboy must know that his immersion in lust, avarice, fame or all three together cannot satisfy his endless seeking for relief of his boredom.

As the term *spirituality* is used today, it often refers vaguely to the nonmaterial aspects of human life and especially to hopes and aspirations, sometimes with little or no moral implications of right or wrong. We find New Age claims, with their eclectic and uncritical terms, that have no connection with the real world. *Force* with a capital *F* is one such term. We find assertions with no intelligent evidence.

Animism in Africa and early Native American religions, while more respectable, are other examples of spiritualities where critical thinking is absent. We are not questioning the good will of these peoples, and we gladly acknowledge that they show that the human mind and heart cannot be satisfied by visible reality alone. But need for the transcendent, the divine, can be satisfied only by the solid, historical and public revelation found in the Old and New Testaments, and most of all in the person and teaching of the Word made flesh, Jesus himself.

GOSPEL LIVING

The word *spirituality* in the Catholic community refers to how the gospel is to be lived in a particular state of life. Thus people think and speak of lay spirituality, married spirituality and priestly spirituality.

This usage is extended to religious orders and congregations and to the various emphases they bring to highlight the endless richness found in Jesus and in his message. Thus the Benedictine order pays particular attention to the liturgy, the Franciscans to poverty and joy, the Dominicans to proclaiming the contemplated Word, the Carmelites to the deep intimacies with the Trinity found in contemplative prayer, the Passionists to the sufferings and death of Jesus. Further examples abound.

The last thing the great founders of religious communities had in mind was to draw attention to themselves as models of holiness. Always their consuming concern was the incarnate Lord, who is "the Way, the Truth and the Life" (John 14:6).

Saint Francis of Assisi was adamant in his desire that the friars and nuns simply imitate Jesus in his radical teaching and way of life. The aim of Saints Teresa of Avila and John of the Cross was to relive the Lord's habitual and long prayerful solitudes, absorbed in the Father, and thus to be of service to the troubled Church of their day.

So it was with Dominic, Ignatius, Francis de Sales, John Bosco, Paul of the Cross and many others through the centuries. While these men and women found other models in Scripture, always towering above them was the figure of Jesus. Their consuming concern was to fashion the lives of their communities on his life and to drink of his teaching.

To be valid, therefore, a Catholic spirituality must embrace all of Scripture. It must be aimed at Trinitarian intimacy, centered on the incarnate Word with his Father and their Holy Spirit. All states in life and all religious communities, Vatican II declared, are to be committed to contemplative intimacy with the Trinity and are to subordinate their work to this contemplation (see *Sacrosanctum Concilium,* 2). Every spirituality must place the passion, death and resurrection of Jesus at its center and see his cross "as God's power to save" (1 Corinthians 1:18).

Jesus' mother, the perfect disciple and the most beautiful of all women, must also be at center stage, for there can be no human son without the mother. The Eucharist is central, and therefore the Mass is the pinnacle of each day.

Without exception, all of us must pursue incessantly a deep conversion, not only from mortal sin but also from venial faults. Every spirituality must lead to heroic virtues, with no mingling of mediocrity or corner cutting in one's aim to give everything to God and in aiding others to do likewise. This must entail our "[giving] up everything that does not lead to God, and all our worldly ambitions" (Titus 2:12). Everyone must embrace our pilgrim status in the supreme journey, aimed as it is at the enthrallment of the beatific vision in the risen body.

FOR ONE AND ALL

If members of a religious order stress one of these essentials to the neglect of other essentials, they have begun to stray. When they give more attention to their founders than to the Lord himself (which can happen), they are straying still further, and their poor founders would be aghast. If they habitually cite and follow their founders selectively (the cafeteria approach), the trouble continues to deepen.

The saints, of course, make none of these mistakes. They embrace divine revelation entirely, and so also the teaching of their Catholic mother. They have no time for vague, vacuous and unfounded generalities, and they would see as irresponsible a cafeteria approach to the divine message.

As we have elsewhere noted, truth is symphonic. Just as a Mozart concerto needs all of the hundreds of notes, each in its precisely correct position, so also each and every element in the deposit of revelation is part of every spirituality. There is a place, of course, as we have above noted, for a special emphasis in a given order or congregation, but that is to happen without leaving aside the truths of revelation that are meant for everyone.

A further caution is in order. When members of a religious institute speak of its spirituality as being Benedictine or

Dominican or Jesuit, they should take care not to give the impression that their emphasis is exclusive and optional for others. Without this care they may be suggesting that one can take that particular truth or leave it without harm. That interpretation is contrary both to the gospel and to Catholic teaching.

We may illustrate the point positively and with an example. Carmelite friars, nuns and secular order members are correct in saying that contemplative prayer is their emphasis. They are right to rejoice that Saints John of the Cross and Teresa of Avila have been declared doctors of the universal Church for their superb explanations of this intimacy with the indwelling Trinity: what it is, how it grows to the summit of the transforming union, what are the conditions of its growth and much else. But Carmelites should also insist that this contemplation is Catholic spirituality and not only Carmelite, and as such it is meant for everyone in the Church. That deep prayer is not optional is clear both in Scripture and in our twenty-century tradition.

The saints, including the saintly founders, happily belong to all of God's people. With their great diversities of culture, personality, talent, age and charisms, they provide to all of us pictures of the endless riches of Jesus and his revelation. There are emphases, yes, but not competition among the movements and spiritualities in the mystical body of Christ. Truth is one magnificent, harmonious and beautiful whole.

CHAPTER TEN
Saints Light Fires

AMONG THE MANY TRAITS THAT SET THE GOSPEL (ROOTED IN Old Testament revelation) apart from and beyond any other worldview is that there is no place in it for mediocrity. Our discussions thus far have encountered totality everywhere: outlooks, attitudes, decisions and self-giving. In the Master and those who follow him closely, there is no room for half measures or lukewarm living (see Revelation 3:1–3, 14–19).

No surprise, therefore, that the saints' impact on world history has been and will continue to be that of setting others on fire. Now, these must be people who are "combustible"— that is, open to being set on fire. It is no secret that God forces himself on no one. If in our willed choices we opt for corner cutting and mediocrity, that is what we shall have—together perhaps with an inclination to do something still more lamentable. Anyone who ponders the matter can see that deliberate venial sins ready a person to slip into deadly mortal sins.

Jesus was crystal clear: "I came to cast fire upon the earth; and would that it were already kindled!" (Luke 12:49, *RSV*). We find the burning motif elsewhere in the New Testament as well. On Resurrection Day, when the Lord joined the two disciples on the road to Emmaus, he explained to them the Scriptures that pertained to himself and foretold his rising from the dead. He then celebrated the Eucharist with them. The impact of the encounter was unforgettable, and when he had vanished from their sight, "they said to each other, 'Did not our hearts burn within us while he talked to us on the road?' " (Luke 24:32, *RSV*).

Later the infant Church gathered in the Upper Room for a forty-day retreat of continuous prayer, which prepared them for the momentous experience of receiving the outpouring of the Holy Spirit. "And there appeared to them tongues as of fire, distributed and resting on each one of them. And they were all filled with the Holy Spirit and began to speak in other tongues, as the Spirit gave them utterance" (Acts 2:3–4, *RSV*). The apostles were transformed by the experience; indeed, metaphorically they were set on fire.

On another occasion in the early Church, when a group of the faithful were at prayer, "the place in which they were gathered together was shaken; and they were all filled with the Holy Spirit and spoke the word of God with boldness" (Acts 4:31, *RSV*). Even though in this text there is no mention of tongues of fire, the experience has rightly been called the little Pentecost, for the effects of this bestowal of power were mighty.

John Henry Newman, the great English convert, was both a brilliant thinker and an avid devotee of ecclesiastical history, especially of the patristic era and of Protestantism from its beginnings to his own day. Among his numerous and original insights was the remark that large groups of people do not light fires in minds and hearts. It is individuals on fire who spark others.

History and contemporary experience furnish us with an abundance of examples. In the secular order parliaments, congresses, legislatures, labor unions and fraternal organizations on occasion offer helpful ideas and solutions to human problems, but there is scant evidence that they ignite conflagrations of burning love and heroic virtue. This is true also in ecclesial organizations.

One might object that Vatican Council II sparked a goodly number of salutary changes in the Church. True enough; its teachings have triggered many needed changes, initiatives and movements among the faithful. But a general council is a special case of the universal Church's operating with the promised assistance of the Holy Spirit: "He who hears you hears me" (Luke 10:16, *RSV*). Lesser groups do not necessarily have that promise.

I may illustrate from recent developments in the institutes of consecrated life. In recent decades general and provincial chapters (elected representatives who set policy in a religious institute) and regional and provincial assemblies have not, as far as one can tell from available evidence, lighted fires. In fact, recent chapters have at times brought religious institutes into a state of crisis by multiple mitigations, though they are never described as mitigations.

For example, there has been the lessening or dropping altogether of meditative and contemplative prayer requirements that the founder or foundress had stipulated. Some have omitted the requirement of a set amount of spiritual reading each day and neutralized the factual frugality required by the vow of poverty. Obedience to the Holy Father as their first religious superior, explicitly included in their vow by canon law, is not enforced in many orders.[1] The most notorious example of this last observation is the widespread refusal to correct numerous liturgical violations that institutes and the faithful generally continue to suffer.

What a chapter or assembly or meeting may sometimes do is smother an initiative sparked by an individual who does happen to be on fire. There are, of course, a number of ways in which this can be done, one of which is to keep a particular issue off a meeting agenda. In this way negative evidence does not have to be faced. These problems occur in marriages as well as in religious life.

FIRE OF THE SPIRIT

What I wish to do at the moment is to suggest positive examples of Newman's insight that it is the saints who light fires. The history of Christ's Church abounds with examples, but let's start at the beginning. Because the phenomena of Pentecost are well known to most of our readers, we will simply refresh our minds with a brief sketch.

Twelve men, who were previously weak and burdened with common human failings, were transformed by the power of the Holy Spirit. As far as we can tell, they then set off in all directions from the Upper Room. In their arduous travels they enjoyed immense success in converting profoundly pagan societies. Happily they gave their lives in cruel martyrdoms because they loved their Lord and the revolutionary message he gave them to proclaim. They lighted fires.

The men and women these apostles converted individually and communally continued these works, likewise with immense success. They too lighted fires. In a nutshell this is the history of the infant Catholic Church. The world had never seen anything like it.

From among the patristic giants I once again choose Augustine, a giant among giants. As we have seen, this model of burning conversion was gifted with a brilliant mind, a rare literary talent, a marvelous humility and zeal, all rooted in heroic love for God and his people. He was remarkable in his pioneering ability to analyze and describe the workings of the human mind and the ability to know. He likewise enjoyed the rare talents of recalling, understanding and wisely applying the vast resources of sacred Scripture to the most arcane problems.

Yet more important than these natural assets was Augustine's ardent search for eternal Triune Beauty. This fiery pursuit of his Master, begun before his conversion, seeps through his masterpieces. To illustrate how simply and yet profoundly this saint could spark anyone even moderately intent on pursuing God, I invite the reader to ponder for a few moments the two following gems. Each of them contains a wealth of theological truth and beauty waiting to be mined by prayerful reflection: "A man possesses the Holy Spirit to the measure of his love for Christ's Church." "O Beauty, so ancient, and so new, too late have I loved you."[2]

It is not surprising that the author of these jewels continues after fifteen centuries to sell in paperback editions. By the written word he continues to ignite fires with his love and light.

Saint Bernard of Clairvaux is a second example. This man of towering talent was extraordinary from his youth on to his mature years. Bruno Scott James, in his introduction to a volume of the saint's letters, tells us that Bernard did not enter the monastery alone: He brought with him no less than thirty companions. "In the way that Bernard induced so many of his noble companions to undertake with him such a hard and rough manner of life we encounter for the first time an indication of that extraordinary power of moving others which was to be characteristic of him all through his life."[3]

Even if we knew nothing further about this young man, one would have to conclude that there was much more to him than natural gifts of personality, though these no doubt were also present. If a candidate for an austere religious order persuaded four or five other men to join him in this demanding enterprise, we would be amazed. But Bernard brought thirty! And he was only twenty-two years old at the time. Still more astonishing is the fact that in three years this comparative youngster would be commissioned to found another monastery in a wilderness. Speak of lighting fires!

The main point of all this is that Bernard was a man of burning love—for God and thus for others. He loved so much that he could speak fearlessly the unpopular truth to a superior or to a group. John the Evangelist tells us that "perfect love casts out fear" (1 John 4:18, *RSV*), and so it was that this saint one day wrote, "It is much more easy to find many men of the world who have been converted from evil to good than it is to find one religious who has progressed from good to better. Anyone who has risen even a little above the state he has once attained in religion is a very rare bird indeed."[4] (We note that this shocking and dim fact is true not only of religious but also of laypeople and clergy.)

One could cite other gems from Bernard's lips and pen, but a few comments about him will have to suffice, this one from the pen of historian G.R. Evans: "Bernard loved the Church with a fierce, protective love.... His immediate and wholehearted response to the Church's needs was all of a piece with the fierceness of his concentration upon God in contemplation."[5] And the prayer of the Church has elegantly captured the firelight of this remarkable man: "Blessed Bernard, your life, flooded by the splendor of the divine Word, illumines the Church with the light of true faith and doctrine."[6]

The great founders of religious orders—Saints Benedict, Dominic, Francis, Teresa, Ignatius, Alphonsus and others too numerous to name here—have covered the world, both Orient and Occident, with missions, schools, universities, parishes, clinics, hospitals, convents and monasteries full of sublime contemplative intimacy with the Trinity and flaming zeal for good works. If the reader ever wonders what book to choose next for spiritual reading, a biography of any one of these saints would detail what we are speaking about in this chapter, indeed in this entire volume. And if we imitated these men and women, we too would light fires.

Although she was not a foundress, the same must be said of Saint Catherine of Siena. This consecrated laywoman lived her beautiful, love-filled virginity in the midst of the world. She was a miracle of a woman in more ways than one. They who want evidence that this is no exaggeration may find it in any solid historical biography of Catherine. I would recommend especially that of her spiritual director, Blessed Raymond of Capua. It is a charming work, one holy person writing about another for whom he had a profound veneration.

Given who Catherine was and what she accomplished, many of her contemporaries must have entertained for her a similar admiration and reverence. She so combined a remarkably tender love for God and for his people that she, like Bernard, could tell bishops and major superiors of religious orders exactly and yet lovingly what they needed to hear. This genuine feminist had male disciples seven centuries before her present-day counterparts lost some of their deepest womanly beauty in attempting to imitate men. Pope John Paul II, speaking at one of his World Youth Days, paraphrased a remark of Catherine and put our point into one short sentence: "If you are what you should be, you will set the whole world ablaze."[7]

FIRE OF TRUTH

In the supernatural order there are two ways of lighting fires. Thus far we have been emphasizing the power of example as evidence of truth: "By this all men will know that you are my disciples, if you have love for one another" (John 13:35, *RSV*). Heroic love is itself proof that the Incarnation has taken place. God has visited in visible form this planet, which he prepared in astonishingly minute detail for the appearance of human life.[8] And of course, he prepared our earth so exquisitely in order that his Son could appear as one of us. The first reality we know without doubt from science, the second from divine revelation.

The other way saints light fires is by teaching the truth they love so much. Obviously our chapter seven is relevant at this point. What I wish to add here is that there are three types of teachers in the Church who rate explicit mention.

The first are the doctors of the Church—that is, men and women officially designated by the popes as teachers (*doctores*, in Latin), outstanding usually in their academic brilliance and always in their heroic lives. These saints have lighted fires by uniting life and doctrine in a seamless whole. In addition to the patristic giants of whom we have already spoken, there are others such as Bernard, Anselm, Thomas Aquinas, Bonaventure, Robert Bellarmine and Francis de Sales.

The Church has named a second group of eminent teachers, also doctors of the Church, but these did not have academic careers. I speak of Catherine of Siena, Teresa of Avila and Thérèse of Lisieux. These women excelled in understanding divine revelation because they were intelligent and naturally gifted in explaining what they experienced but mainly because of their profound intimacy with God, their heroic holiness and their eager listening to the proclaimed word. These three traits triggered insights that lesser folks simply do not enjoy.

The third type of saint to light fires is the hidden one, the one not widely known as a brilliant beacon. Immediately the Curé of Ars, Saint John Vianney, comes to mind. As we have already noted, this priest, in the anonymity of the confessional, brought light and healing to numberless people through the sacrament and by his love and wisdom. In other hidden ways saintly teachers in classrooms, spouses at home and workers in shops and offices scatter light through their sheer goodness wherever they are.

SOME THEOLOGICAL CONCLUSIONS

We may now ask, just why is sanctity so lightsome? Normal people are attracted to holiness, often strongly attracted. Crowds of townspeople flocked to get a glimpse of Saint Teresa of Avila when on rare occasions she would leave her cloister to found a new monastery. In our day other crowds typically surrounded Blessed Teresa of Calcutta.

All this should be no surprise, for heroic sanctity is the greatest beauty of the human person. Beauty sheds light, a fascinating, alluring light.[9] It often moves receptive people more than reason does, even solid reason based on solid evidence—which, of course, is light of another type. Personal beauty and intellectual confirmation together are doubly powerful in drawing people to the truth.

There remains a die-hard idea, current among some clergy and laity, that despite compelling biblical and magisterial statements to the contrary, there is either an uneasy truce or a positive clash between apostolic commitment and prayerful solitude. We have heard it said that communal prayer and contemplative intimacy with the Trinity are monastic enterprises and thus have no primary place in the diocesan priesthood and apostolic orders and among other hardworking people. In this view we gather in community to get a job done. Not a few men and women who should know Scripture better continue to hold this antiquated idea.

Why antiquated and false? The questions these people should ask are not whether communal prayer and contemplative intimacy with God are monastic, but are they biblical? The answer is a thundering yes.[10] Consider the habitual, long, prayerful solitudes of Jesus and then of the Church's greatest apostles.

The intrinsic relationship between action and contemplation, work and prayer, is well expressed in a neat medieval formula: "*Ex plenitude contemplationis activus*—active, working from a fullness of contemplation." These few words mean that in all states of life—whether one is a bishop, priest, monk, nun, husband or wife, single or widowed—the fulfillment of our duties of state and apostolic work should spring from a deep contemplative union with God. This is a consistent theism and common sense, which unfortunately is not always common.

Vatican Council II was even more pointed when it remarked that priests should work *ex abundantia contemplationis,* "from an abundance of contemplation, to the delight of the whole Church of God" (*Lumen Gentium,* 41).[11] This of course applies to everyone in each state of life, for in this question there are no distinctions among vocations.

Finally we should notice that these two conciliar statements do not simply state that all of us should work zealously and pray deeply, nor do they merely repeat the classic idea that our work should be an overflow of contemplation (both of which are true). More forcefully they tell us that contemplative intimacy *begets* action, makes it to be. There is not the least hint of a clash. On the contrary we have still another illustration that truth is a marvelous symphony of splendor. Indeed, saints light fires.

But let's remember too that contemplation is not simply a means to action. It is an end in itself, just as genuine love is. This intimacy with God is the top priority in human life, the "one thing" of Psalm 27:4 and Luke 10:38–42. Vatican II recalled this same basic truth: In the Church action is directed and subordinated to contemplation (see *Sacrosanctum Concilium,* 2).

The saints live this symphonic beauty and thus are strong and fearless. Their motivation is pure in whatever they do and say. Led by the Spirit, they are faithful to the Lord and to his Church. They are love-lights in our dark world of mediocrity and even outrageous crime. In the saints, and most of all in her Founder and his Mother, the Church is triumphant.

CHAPTER ELEVEN
Icons of Human Love

IN EXAMINING THE SAINTS AS MODELS OF HUMAN LOVE, WE need to identify more precisely what this love is and is not. Let's begin with the latter and clear away possible misunderstandings.

Genuine Christian love is not merely a feeling of warm affection for a blood relation or a close friend, good as that feeling is. Nor is it simply a need relationship, even if the needs are mutual. After all, needs come and go, while love, real love, does not end.

Furthermore, contrary to the endless messages of the media, print and electronic, love is not attraction, noble or ignoble. We should appreciate beauty, but that inclination can be thoroughly egocentric. Attraction is common, but so is egocentrism. Lust is also common—and completely self-centered, the exact opposite of love.

But then what is real love? It is a willed, self-sacrificing giving to another, even if attraction and feelings are absent, and even if little or nothing is received in return. Genuine love appeared on earth in splendid beauty in the incarnate Word of the Father, who "so loved the world that he gave his only-begotten Son" (John 3:16, *RSV*). The perfect icon of love is Jesus crucified: He gave the most complete love and received rejection in return. After the example of the Master, this is how saints love.

Several conclusions follow. The first is that it takes deep conversion and a lofty sanctity to love deeply. We must be purified of numberless egocentrisms to live the reality we have just traced. We find this truth plainly taught in the First Letter of Peter: To love others sincerely and from the heart, a person must accept and live divine revelation and be purified in mind and will (see 1 Peter 1:22–23). And as I explained in chapter four, this purification flows from a profound intimacy with the Trinity. Such is how the saints love so perfectly even unattractive people—yes, enemies included.

A second conclusion is that there is no such thing as love at first sight. There is, of course, attraction at first sight, hopefully noble and honorable: attractions not only to physical comeliness but also to charming personality, intellectual competence and noble character. But as I have already noted, attraction, even strong attraction, is not yet love. Genuine love demands sacrifice; it is permanent and self-giving, not merely receiving. The saints are givers, not takers.

How then do the saints love other people: old and young, beautiful and ugly, talented and dull, pleasant and grouchy, good and bad? They are selfless and self-giving.

Think of the great missionaries: Boniface, Francis Xavier, Junípero Serra, Peter Chanel. These and a host of others left their homes and lands to live in trying circumstances. Some were brutally murdered for their troubles.

Then there are women like Catherine of Siena, Clare of Assisi, Teresa of Avila and Thérèse of Lisieux. These experienced many trials, small and huge. Rather than get discouraged and disgusted with the wickedness of this world, they healed what was wrong by forgiving and loving in action, not merely in words.

The love of these heroic ones burned because it originated in their enduring love for God and prayerful intimacy with Triune Beauty. Without divine grace and determined motivation, no one can live on their level. Saints live lives of love.

SAINTS AND SUFFERING

Genuine human love manifests itself most bravely in the whats and whys and hows of the sufferings that come upon all humans sooner or later. Handling suffering well seems to be among the last lessons most of us learn in our lives. Indeed, some unfortunates seem to know little about handling it wisely.

I am thinking not only of the hardships of illnesses, accidents, failures and inclement weather. Even more do I envision the deepest and most frequent hurts and pains we meet in our pilgrim journey, those due to sin and a lack of deep conversion: bickering, loveless indifference, verbal and physical abuse, calculated betrayals, egocentric avarice and lust. Unfortunately, we need to add to this depressing list brutal, hate-filled and wanton terrorism, together with tyranny, injustice and religious persecution.

Why does our infinitely powerful and good God permit these atrocities? This is not the place to answer this question completely. The reader may consult Pope John Paul II's light-filled and salutary apostolic letter on the subject, *Salvifici Doloris*. Here we shall consider one essential reason why God permits evils in our world: the preservation of human freedom. If we were to demand that God prevent one sin, why not a thousand or all of them? But then there would be no human freedom, no human persons, no love, no happiness, no eternal life, no saints. What we would be asking for is a race of robots and machines, not persons.

From the outset we need to notice that suffering does not automatically improve a person. How and why we suffer matter immensely. If we become cynical and bitter in the afflictions that come our way, we are becoming worse, not better. Not only are we being diminished as persons, complaining and grouchy toward others and ourselves, but also we are suffering over and over again from our repeated rehashing of the causes of our pains.

If, however, we respond to the blows and buffets of life in union with the Lord, in his suffering and death out of love for us, we grow rapidly in both holiness and joy. The picture of Jesus on the cross is at once the unparalleled horror and the superlative beauty in our universe. A crucifix portrays supreme ugliness because it is a picture of grave sin rejecting and tormenting infinite Splendor, and yet it is the consummate beauty because it portrays perfect love, even for the loveless. Hans Urs von Balthasar has remarked that "it is face to face with Christ crucified that the abysmal egoism of what we are accustomed to call love becomes clear."[1]

The saints live faithfully the only ultimate answer to the problem of suffering: the passion, death and resurrection of the incarnate Word of the Father. Martyrs go to their tortures and brutal executions with joy, love and forgiveness of enemies because they love their Lord with complete abandon. A New Testament illustration of this marvelous love is Saint Stephen in Acts 7:59–60.

The *Roman Martyrology* offers hundreds more. And we see such martyrs even today, the victims of atheistic regimes and of religious fanaticism.

LOVE IN ACTION

The saints teach us by their actions as well as by their words not only why they suffer so willingly but also how to live in and through the vicissitudes of life. They will have no part in the world's retaliations, major or minor: "If you snap at me or are cold toward me, I will snap back at you and treat you with indifference, if not hatred." Retaliation compounds evils in the home, the shop, the office and, yes, on an international scale as well. Our daily papers and the evening news abound in painful evidences.

Saints relive the virile gentleness of Jesus, who never retaliated in response to the most outrageous abuses our planet has ever seen. Saint Paul encapsulated the Christlike solution to the problem of evil in three statements in his Letter to the Romans. We are, he said, to bless those who persecute us and never curse them. We are never to repay evil with evil, but rather to respond with noble and kindly thoughts and deeds. And the overall divine course of action is to overcome evil with good (see Romans 12:14, 17, 21).

Consider Saint Peter Claver, who tenderly cared for black slaves disembarking to pitiful conditions on South American shores. So full of divinized human love for them was Peter that he vowed to be "the slave of the blacks forever." You can read an account of this exquisite love in the *Liturgy of the Hours* for Saint Peter's feast day, September 9.[2]

While giving lectures to Missionaries of Charity in Calcutta, I was privileged to see with my own eyes their care for the "poorest of the poor." The plight of the impoverished people they serve in the slums was appalling. On Christmas Day, to give one example of many, I witnessed two long lines, one of men and another of women, pitifully destitute, hungry and ill, all invited to the nuns' compound for a bountiful Christmas dinner, complete with second servings. Everyone was welcome, with no questions asked, Catholics but also Protestants, Hindus and Muslims. The crowd was huge.

I am canonizing no one, but these women and their lay helpers looked very much like the people we are discussing in this book. They loved in action and not only in words. I shall never forget what I saw.

CHAPTER TWELVE
Masterpieces of Beauty

MOST PEOPLE RECOGNIZE BEAUTY WHEN THEY SEE OR HEAR IT: an orchid, an oak tree, a bluebird, a lovely face, a Mozart concerto. Astronomers, microbiologists and theologians who are alive to their tasks may well experience a thrill of delight in the splendor of a newly discovered truth—in the vastness of the universe, the incredible complexity of a living cell or the depths of divine revelation. Yet not a few ordinary folks would be stymied when asked to define just what beauty is.

Hence in order to appreciate more fully the theme of this chapter, I will sketch briefly the classic concept of beauty, which happens also to be in surprising accord with the contemporary thoughts of our best physicists. For a more thorough explanation, the reader may consult my book *The Evidential Power of Beauty*, especially chapters one through six.

There are four elements in the standard analysis of the beautiful: wholeness, proportion, unity and radiant form. A lovely face is whole and complete—that is, nothing essential to a human countenance is missing: Both eyes are present, as are the mouth and nose and ears. There is proportion: Neither the nose nor the mouth is too large or too small. There is unity: All parts of the face are present in their proper places; the nose is not on a cheek.

The deepest root of beauty in a plant, animal or human person is what philosophers call "the radiant form." The word *form* does not refer here first of all to external shape but rather to the essence, the whatness. The form of an orchid is the basic root cause of its particular splendor. The radiant form of a rose is its inner essence, which makes it a rose of this species and not a tulip or a palm tree. Your radiant form is your human soul in your unique body, which determines what kind of being you are. This is the deepest source of your splendor as the pinnacle of the visible universe—the human person.[1]

THE BEAUTY OF THE SAINTS

We are now prepared to ponder the implications of the title of this chapter. How do the men and women we are considering in this book exemplify our classic summary of what beauty is all about? There are several ways in which to respond to this question.

The first is to recall our definition and to apply it to chapters four and five, "Transforming Intimacy," and "Heroic Virtue in Action." The saints are whole and complete as persons, deeply in love and possessing all the virtues. They possess these goodness powers to a heroic degree and thus enjoy a magnificent proportion with love filling their lives without limits. Each of their moral virtues is what a moral virtue is meant to be: a mean between the two extremes of too much or too little when dealing with material things.

The lives of these men and women likewise have a remarkable unity. Their transforming contemplative love binds together into a splendid oneness all of their praying, working, conversing, eating, recreating and resting. The radiant form of their lives, indeed the most radiant of all forms, is the Christ form. They put on the Lord Jesus to the nth degree: "He is the radiant light of God's glory and the perfect copy of his nature" (Hebrews

1:3). Indeed, he is so perfectly the radiant form that he is the very "light of the world," the sole "Way, the Truth and the Life" (John 8:12; 14:6). No other view of the dignity and value of a human person even comes close to the one God conceived.

British writer and television personality Malcolm Muggeridge encountered these traits of beauty while doing a TV documentary at Lourdes. A woman on pilgrimage asked him to see her sick sister.

> The sister was obviously at the point of death, and like any other glib child of twentieth-century enlightenment, I had nothing to say, until I noticed in the most extraordinarily vivid way...that her eyes were quite fabulously luminous and beautiful. "What marvellous eyes!" As I said this, the three of us—the dying woman, her sister, and I—were somehow caught up into a kind of ecstasy. I can't describe it any other way. It was as though I saw God's love shining down on us visibly, in an actual radiance.[2]

This account, coming as it does from a gifted and no-nonsense sort of literary figure, is worth pondering. It reminds me of a letter I received several decades ago from an acquaintance. She wrote of a nun she had met: "She's a woman almost visibly on fire with love; talking to her is like holding the straw of my soul close to the fire."

While these recollections do not deal with canonized saints, they do make it easy to understand the words of Saint Bernard, a man himself on fire: "When I think of them, I feel myself inflamed by a tremendous yearning."[3]

What is it about these men and women that so touches our human capacity to appreciate their splendor? Their heroic, selfless love is beauty in action. I spoke in chapter one of the two types of human excellence: the first being talents, skills and accomplishments; the second being perfection as a person: genuine selfless love, honesty, patience, humility, chastity, gentleness, justice—indeed, everything we are dealing with in this book. While the natural gifts of course are good, even admirable, personal perfection is vastly more important—and more beautiful!

Portraying the splendor of the saints, beauty in action, is beyond the talents and abilities of human artists. Even in its sympathetic films Hollywood is incapable of conveying the inner depths of beauty in the saints. Their charm is of divine origin, a sign of God's doing (see John 13:35). Given that we men and women are "little less than the angels" in our human dignity (Psalm 8:5, *RSV*) and are to be God's works of art, it follows that the heroic ones are his masterpieces.

ALIVE TO BEAUTY

One of the most pervasive illnesses of our contemporary social scene is the lack of wonder at and enthusiasm for the most precious beauties of life. This problem shows itself in sizeable segments of the population both young and old, and it has several names to describe it: dullness, apathy, boredom. Among the chief symptoms of this malaise is a proclivity toward artificial and exaggerated stimuli: clamorous noise, drugs, violence, alcohol, irresponsible sexual indulgences.

Parents who themselves have little sense of wonder at the marvels of our earth and the entire universe are unlikely to spark enthusiasm in their children. The same is true of the still more awesome wonders of the supernatural order of divine revelation. Advanced education in the sciences and in theology should be characterized by an abidingly appreciative delight in the never-ending and amazing surprises that it uncovers.

Biologist Lewis Thomas marveled at how his colleagues in the sciences show so little wonder in what they find in their daily work.

> How it happens that today's scientists remain, by and large, such a steady and unruffled lot, writing their cool, meditative papers just as though what they are reporting are the expected, normal, flat facts of the matter, instead of rushing out of their laboratories into the streets shouting their exultations to the queerness of nature, I shall never know.[4]

Boredom and sanctity are incompatible. Saints live Saint Paul's admonition to "rejoice in the Lord always" (Philippians 4:4, *RSV*), not only in their successes and celebrations but even in the midst of their labors and sufferings. Saint Teresa of Avila was physically ill much of her adult life, and yet she was a happy and fulfilled woman who could delight at the delicately constructed splendor of an insect. Saint John of the Cross could be captivated gazing at the night sky, with his elbows resting on the windowsill of his cell, in deepest intimacy with the indwelling Trinity.

Love bestows sight, and the deepest love triggers the deepest treasuring appreciation of reality. Thomas Howard writes that the English novelist Charles Williams had the gift of seeing the precious value of simple and common things that most people hardly even notice:

SAINTS *A Closer Look*

The eye with which he looked at ordinary things was like the eye of a lover looking at his lady. The lover sees this plain woman crowned with the light of heaven. She walks in beauty. Her eyes are windows of Paradise to him. Her body, every inch of it, is an incarnation and epiphany of celestial grace. In her he finds the ecstatic vision that his heart has sought.

All this passionate intensity, Williams would argue, is not illusion. The ecstatic vision of beauty thus vouchsafed to that lover is true, not false. The lady *is* as glorious as he sees her to be. It has been given to him, the man who loves her, to see the truth about her. The rest of us bystanders, mercifully, have not had our eyes thus opened, else we would all go mad. It would be an intolerable burden of glory if we all saw, unveiled, the splendor of all other creatures, all the time.[5]

CONCLUSIONS

Because the three transcendentals—truth, goodness and beauty—are so intimately intertwined, the saints see the most important truths and aspects of human existence far more clearly and comprehensively than do sinners and the mediocre. Despite their best efforts, the electronic media are unable to portray the inner splendor of the saints, what they are like in the deepest centers of their persons. The reason is that heroic beauty is of heaven, and earthly efforts cannot express it adequately. In this connection I borrow a passage from *The Evidential Power of Beauty:*

In any given age saints are messages from the Lord as to what the world at that moment of history needs especially to hear and to see. They are symphonies of beauty, whole, united, entire, and burning with love. They are teenagers and young adults so loving their virginity and their divine Bridegroom that they gladly surrender their lives rather than permit a violation of their purity. They are martyrs singing for joy and forgiving their murderers with touching love. They are husbands and wives showing the world in their hiddenness how to combine devotion to each other and to their children in hectic everyday occupations with lofty mystical contemplation. They are priests and bishops selflessly emptying themselves for others by day and lost in profound prayer by night. They are indeed works of divine art.[6]

Our final conclusion: Art always requires an artist. Beauty does not and cannot happen by random chance. No random swirling of trillions of atoms and molecules through billions of years of winds and rains could produce in marble the exquisite masterpiece of Michelangelo's *Pietà*. Neither will a Beethoven symphony or a rose or the far greater marvel of a human person happen by chance. It would be absurd to suggest that the waltzes of Johann Strauss occurred by pouring thousands of tiny cardboard notes onto a gymnasium floor.

Take a bag of thousands of letters of the alphabet, shake them up and then pour them out. Seldom will you find three juxtaposed letters spelling out one word, *cat* or *try,* for example. Rare indeed would be a five-letter word, almost never one of twelve letters. Mathematicians point out that getting one intelligible sentence of twenty-five words by mere chance is fantastically unlikely. Outrageously impossible would it be to discover a volume of the complete works of Charles Darwin or William Shakespeare born of random shakings.

Saintly splendor happens through two intellects and two free wills, those of the divine Artist and of the human saying yes to the gifts he gives. Saints have the habit of saying yes, sinners the habit of saying no.

CHAPTER THIRTEEN
Glories of Catholicism

I RECEIVED A LETTER FROM A CONVERT WHO WONDERED whether our Protestant friends have saints. I should like to broaden this question to include members of non-Christian religions: Do they also count in their membership men and women of heroic virtue with the profound intimacy of God that we have been discussing in these pages?

Scholars in the various Christian and non-Christian communities would be more likely than I to know if there are well-documented studies similar to the rigorous Catholic beatification and canonization processes. Popular reports of unusual deeds do not, of course, establish this heroism in all the virtues. That being noted, I offer a few comments that can contribute to answering the question raised by our convert.

No one wishes to suggest that other Christian communities lack members who are admirable in loving God and others in him. The Lord continues, after all, to work in anyone who pursues honesty and moral rectitude. This is ordinary Catholic teaching. He is working also in the hearts of the sincere men and women in non-Christian religions, even though they lack the sublime revelation that, among other gifts, contains the seven sacramental channels of grace and the divine promises given to Peter and his successors.

At the same time the saints are more than sincere and honest and devoted. They are, as Saint Paul observes, a new creation, a revolution, well described by our terms *heroes* and *heroines* (see Ephesians 4:23–24). They are extraordinarily beautiful, divine masterpieces. In our canonization processes the Lord chooses to share his judgment concerning these moral miracles. He confirms this judgment with thoroughly investigated, scientifically scrutinized, physical miracles.

Because of their sheer attractiveness, the saints are powerful ads for Catholicism. They live the Church's teachings and her life to the hilt. That, put simply, is why they are so fulfilled. We recall in this context the emphatic reaction of Edith Stein when putting down the autobiography of Saint Teresa: "This is the truth!"[1]

In like manner biographer Thomas Walsh remarked that a Church that can produce a Teresa of Avila must be the true Church. Chinese intellectual John Wu came to the same conclusion about Thérèse of Lisieux. Indeed, where else on our planet do we find the likes of Augustine, Bernard, Aquinas, Catherine, Robert Bellarmine, the Curé of Ars and a host of others?

THE CHURCH ON TRIAL

Criticism and conflicts have a long history in our various human societies, both civil and ecclesial. Contentions and discord began with Adam and Eve and their immediate descendants, but with our current mass media—both print and electronic—negative quarreling has reached a saturation point. Political parties are continually at odds with one another. Nations criticize one another and only too often resort to war to settle their disagreements. Terrorists refuse even to dialogue, and some, in the name of God, wantonly kill large numbers of innocent children and adults in expressing their fanatical hatreds.

The only honest and fair way to evaluate an organization or a movement, secular or religious, is to judge it according to the performance of members who accept its aims, teachings and principles and live them faithfully. It is not fair, for example, to judge communism on the basis of those who reject the teachings of Marx and Lenin and do not live by them. Neither are dissenting and "cafeteria" Catholics examples of what their Church is about and what she teaches. Any human community will have some number of mediocre and renegade members.

It is difficult to imagine a person who studied this sort of matter more brilliantly and thoroughly than G.K. Chesterton, and it was he who remarked that as soon as a person begins to be fair to the Catholic Church, he begins to love her. It was no surprise therefore that after his conversion, he loved his newly found home so vastly, even touchingly.

I should like to think that in commending the saints with the title of this chapter, it would be obvious that we are not patting ourselves on the back. We are praising God, from whom comes every good and perfect gift (see James 1:17). All the same, it is true that these holy ones are men and women who say an emphatic yes to the divine Artist and thus are free of damaging defects.

In the last chapter we considered beauty. Here we ponder for a few moments just what it is that mars any beautiful object, whether in art, nature or the supernatural. A painting of a human face with eyes placed on the cheeks, the nose on the chin and the ears where the eyes should be is ugly. A sleek new automobile with its parts haphazardly strewn on a garage floor has lost its appeal. In matters of truth and intellectual endeavor (astronomy, microbiology, medicine, philosophy, theology), conflicts, errors and contradictions distort reality and therefore erode its beauty.

So it is with morality, religion and politics. Disagreements are frequent in these three fields, not usually because there is a lack of evidence as to where the truth lies but because these areas have an immediate impact on how people want to live. When a moral, religious or political issue touches on personal property or money, sexuality, power, recreation, duties and obligations, we should expect disagreements.

The most radical and deep divisions among us are rooted not in our minds but in our free will. When a selfish person wants something to satisfy his egocentric desires, licit or illicit, intellectually based evidence against his position counts for little or nothing. His desires trump a concern for truth.

In these matters of morality and religion, Jesus well knew the wounded nature and vagaries of the human mind and will, and so he wisely gifted his Church with plain signs of where any honest seeker can discover his complete message. We call these signs the four marks of the Church—that is, indicators of where Christ's authentic teachings can be securely found until the end of time.

HITTING THE MARKS

How do the saints fit into this picture? They are the visible models of these four marks of the community Jesus founded: apostolicity, unity, universality and holiness. All four are "inseparably linked with each other [Cf. DS 2888]" (*CCC*, 811; see also 750, 825–826, 865).

The mark of apostolicity means that the Church of Christ must and does historically go back to the twelve apostles, with

Peter and his successors as their head. Jesus explicitly promised that he would be with the Church he established "always; yes, to the end of time" (Matthew 28:20). All the saints have clung tenaciously to this hierarchical structure, even to the point of dying gruesome deaths in fidelity to it. Saint Thomas More comes to mind as an excellent example. Saint Ignatius of Antioch, about the year 110, was eloquent on this subject of the centrality of the Roman see. He wrote to the Romans: "Yes, you rank first in love, being true to Christ's law and stamped with the Father's name."[2]

Jesus addressed the second mark, unity, at the Last Supper, when he prayed to the Father that his followers would be "completely one" in doctrine, government, community and holiness (see John 17:21, 23). This gift is of course bound together with that of apostolicity, deriving as it does from the promises to Peter and the other apostles, teaching in union with him, and their successors. In our fractious and wayward human race, oneness of mind and heart in what matters most is otherwise impossible. Twenty centuries of history, with the approximately twenty-seven thousand different Christian groups that have evolved over that time, make this perfectly clear.

Dissenters who reject magisterial teaching do not destroy this unity, even though they can and often do inflict no little pain on other people. As Jewish writer Will Herberg pointed out, no movement in Catholic history has had lasting success if it has been opposed to or been unsupported by the papal office. History illustrates theology.

The saints have through the centuries (and to our own day) treasured this divinely assured oneness to the point of suffering brutal martyrdoms on its behalf. Already in the third century Saint Cyprian, himself a bishop and a martyr, celebrated in one of his letters the glories of his fellow victim victors:

> How blessed is this Church of ours, so honored and illuminated by God and ennobled in these our days by the glorious blood of martyrs! In earlier times it shone white with the good deeds of our brethren, and now it is adorned with the red blood of martyrs. It counts both lilies and roses among its garlands. Let each of us, then, strive for the highest degree of glory, whichever be the honor for which he is destined; may all Christians be found worthy of either the pure white crown of a holy life or the royal red crown of martyrdom.[3]

In the same letter Cyprian marveled while extolling the fidelity of these heroes under the fiercest tortures. They were "so mangled that no whole members [of their bodies] were left to suffer punishment." Gifted with divine strength, these "tortured men stood there stronger than their torturers; battered and lacerated limbs triumphed over clubs and claws that tore them."[4]

The third mark of the Lord's Church, universality, adds additional luster to the beauty of these intertwined gifts. The community Jesus founded has spread throughout the earth, even though in a few lands violent persecutions continue to force the faithful to go underground.

HOLINESS

Throughout this study we have been analyzing and explaining the fourth mark of the Church, holiness. Extraordinary women and men—yes, even children and teenagers—have been open to the light of truth and the power of the seven sacraments within the apostolicity, universality and unity of this one bride of Christ, who "loved the Church and sacrificed himself for her to make her holy" (Ephesians 5:25–26). Chapters four and five, on transforming intimacy and heroic virtue, bear upon these glories of Jesus' community. Even though, as Jesus also made clear, there would be chaff mingled with the wheat, he gave us clear signs of how the two can be distinguished.

The same beauties of holiness in apostolic unity can be noticed also in the intimate and burning sentiments expressed by saintly minds and hearts. While we have seen a few examples of these outpourings, I add here two more illustrations.

The first comes from the pen of Saint Teresa. While in her humility she was not inclined to share the profound favors she received from "His Majesty," we are blessed that she obeyed those who asked her to do so. In her *Soliloquies* she addressed her own soul:

> O life, life! How can you endure being separated from your Life? In so much solitude, with what are you occupied? What are you doing, since all your works are imperfect and faulty?... O Lord, how gentle are Your ways!... [W]hen I set out to serve You, I find nothing that proves a satisfactory payment for anything of what I owe. It seems I want to be completely occupied in Your service....
>
> O my God and my Mercy! What shall I do so as not to undo the great things You've done for me? Your works are holy, they are just, they are priceless....[5]

This woman was obviously head over heels in love with the Lord.

Our second illustration comes from a man with a very different personality but also deeply in love: Saint John Vianney, the Curé of Ars:

I love You, O my God, and my sole desire is to love You until the last breath of my life. I love You, O infinitely lovable God, and I prefer to die loving You than live one instant without loving You.... O my God, if my tongue cannot say in every moment that I love You, I want my heart to say it in every beat. Allow me the grace to suffer loving You, to love You suffering and one day to die loving You and feeling that I love You. And as I approach my end, I beg You to increase and perfect my love of You.[6]

We do well to recall that these ardent protestations are light years removed from egocentric infatuations—which is to say that they are divinely given and received. Hence it should be unnecessary to remark that Teresa and the Curé, indeed all the saints, match their words with their deeds. With them there is no gap between their professions at prayer and their choices in the nitty-gritty of daily life.

BEAUTY AND TRUTH

As we discussed earlier, anyone who is free of materialistic orthodoxies knows that random chance does not and cannot produce a work of art: literature, painting, sculpture, music. There are over thirty thousand species of orchids, each a masterpiece. These must come from a supreme Artist. Yet far beyond all the glorious flowers on this earth, the saints are God's supreme works of art.

We know that the beauty of Christ is spectacularly evident in the lives of the saints. This dazzling beauty is evident, that is, to anyone whose vision is clear of egocentrism. Indeed, beauty possesses a remarkable evidential power. Each saint is a beacon of light and truth.

As I mentioned earlier, this is not only sound theology but also sound science. Our best and most original and creative scientists agree that beauty is a sure pointer to truth. In support of this statement I share here a few lines from one of my earlier works, *The Evidential Power of Beauty:*

> In their fascinating book *The New Story of Science,* Robert Augros and George Stanciu develop the growing conviction that in the sciences, and perhaps most of all in physics, beauty is considered to be a powerful pointer to the truth of a theory....
>
> "All of the most eminent physicists of the twentieth century agree that beauty is the primary standard for scientific truth."... [Nobel Prize winner] Richard Feynman...remarked that "you can recognize truth by its beauty and simplicity." Equally well known and respected as a founder of quantum mechanics, Werner Heisenberg has written that the truth of his theory "was immediately found convincing by virtue of its completeness and abstract beauty."...
>
> Another Nobel laureate, Paul Dirac, noted for his work on the question of quantum mechanics and relativity [stated]: "It is more important to have beauty in one's equations than to have them fit experiment."[7]

This striking convergence of contemporary science with centuries of our best theology is one of a number of intersections (the big bang is another) worthy of close examination by scholars in both fields. For our purposes here we have more convincing evidence supporting what we are explaining about the beauty of the saints. They are immediately convincing. In the heroism of their selfless loving without limit, we see reflections of divine loveliness. As von Balthasar has observed, beauty also points to infinity. Indeed it does.

MOTHER OF THE SAINTS

Now we apply our excursion into physics to the point of this present chapter. Yes, the community of the canonized ones is blessed with the most attractive, selfless, compelling and convincing people on earth. To put the matter in a summarizing nutshell, the saints are men and women on fire, totally self-giving even to enemies, alive and vivacious, thoroughly honest and authentic, profoundly happy even in suffering, heroic in patience, humility, chastity and love. They surpass our human capabilities, which is why they are miracles of goodness, moral miracles.

Now, how does all this happen? Saints do not drop out of the blue. Why do they flourish in the Church Jesus founded?

There are a number of answers to these crucial questions. The first is that this Church, by the explicit promise of her Founder, proclaims through all the centuries the whole of what he had to say, the entirety of divine revelation—nothing suppressed, no corner cutting, no compromises with what the world at any given time wants to hear and do. Hearing this undiluted message, these heroic ones gladly embrace it in its totality. What could Infinite Beauty do but pour out his own beauty upon them?

We can break this answer down into some specifics. A saint is a woman or a man who lives fully what the Church is and teaches. Truth transforms; it is real. Euphemisms, on the other hand, transform no one. "Pro-choice" is not a rallying cry of selfless, heroic people, and no one is the least tempted to think so.

Further, the Church's seven sacraments, themselves issuing from the will of her Lord, are powerhouses of holiness for those who receive them well. Coming from Jesus himself, what else could they be?

The sacrament of reconciliation, commonly called confession, forgives guilt because he said it would: "Whose sins you forgive, they are forgiven" (John 20:23). The sentence could not be more explicit. This sacrament heals our wounded, sinful nature and gives us the strength to do better in the future. It offers occasions for one-on-one advice on how to do better.

In the divinely instituted Eucharist Jesus comes that we might have life and have it abundantly (see John 10:10). This is why anyone who cares to notice can see numerous men and women coming to weekday Masses in the dead of winter as well as in the summer heat. They come to a powerhouse of vitality and strength for the day's duties, responding to the magnificent promise of John's Gospel: "He who eats my flesh and drinks my blood lives in me and I live in him" (John 6:56). The celebration of Mass and its extension into eucharistic adoration is the chief fountain of heroic holiness. It is the high point of every single day, the chief source of the fire Jesus came to cast on the earth.

The third specific answer to the question, "How does heroic holiness happen?" is that monasticism and other forms of consecrated life have through the centuries concretized the evangelical counsels of poverty, chastity and obedience as spurs to going beyond the minimum in all states of life. Our point is not that husbands and wives are called to the same frugality and chastity as religious—they obviously are not—but that they are reminded of their call to the same heights of holiness. History makes it clear that monasticism is a tremendous civilizing force for goodness, holiness and the deepest of beauties.

Our fourth answer is allied with the third: We have in the Church an immensely rich and beautiful heritage of written masterpieces dealing with heroic holiness and intimacy with the Trinity. All rooted in the inspired Word of the Scriptures and enriching one another, these writings come through twenty centuries from the brilliant minds and burning hearts of holy men and women: Augustine, Chrysostom, the Gregorys, Bernard, Thomas Aquinas, Catherine, Teresa, John of the Cross, Thérèse, Newman, von Balthasar and many others. These works inspire others to like devotion.

MESSAGES THE WORLD NEEDS TO HEAR

Whether they are on the right or left or in the middle of the culture and political spectrum, every serious commentator I have heard and read in recent years agrees that our world is in critically precarious circumstances. We assume that most readers need no one to spell out for them the details of this agreement. There is, however, little agreement as to what is to be thought and done politically about these potentially catastrophic problems. I refer, for example, to the apparently growing clash of civilizations.

While there have been saintly kings and politicians, let's consider here what ordinary citizens are to be and to do. We have already made the point that we Christian people are to overcome evil with good, with neither hatred nor retaliation.

Saints are our models in this effort. They are all overcoming evil with good. Unless we the hidden ones are living this and other divine prescriptions for healing, politicians are not going to get very far. Hence, without doubt, what we need in our deeply troubled world at the outset of this new millennium is to have farmers and day laborers, professionals of all sorts, legislators, judges and heads of state come closer and closer to imitating the men and women we celebrate in this volume.

Paul calls us all to "be innocent and genuine, *perfect children of God among a deceitful and underhand brood*," and so we will "shine in the world like bright stars" (Philippians 2:15). Following the saints of all vocations and all careers, we are to be fires of love and beauty in our deeply troubled world.

BIBLIOGRAPHY

Abbott, Walter, ed. *Documents of Vatican II*. New York: America, 1966.

Augustine. *The Trinity*, Edmund Hill, trans. New York: New City, 1996.

Benedict XIV. *The Beatification and Canonization of the Servants of God*. London: Thomas Richardson and Son, 1850.

Catechism of the Catholic Church. Second edition. Vatican City: Libreria Editrice Vaticana, 1997.

Cousins, Ewert, trans. *Bonaventure: The Soul's Journey Into God; The Tree of Life; The Life of St. Francis*. Part of *The Classics of Western Spirituality*. New York: Paulist, 1978.

Dubay, Thomas. *Deep Conversion/Deep Prayer*. San Francisco: Ignatius Press, 2006.

_____. *The Evidential Power of Beauty*. San Francisco: Ignatius, 1999.

_____. *Fire Within: St. Teresa of Avila, St. John of the Cross, and the Gospel—on Prayer*. San Francisco: Ignatius, 1989.

_____. *Prayer Primer: Igniting a Fire Within*. San Francisco: Ignatius, 2002.

Evans, G.R. *The Mind of Saint Bernard of Clairvaux*. Oxford: Oxford University Press, 1983.

Flannery, Austin, ed. *Vatican Council II: Conciliar and Post Conciliar Documents*. Northport, N.Y.: Costello, 1988.

James, Bruno Scott, trans. *The Letters of St. Bernard of Clairvaux*. Chicago: Regnery, 1953.

Kavanaugh, Kieran and Otilio Rodriguez, trans. *The Collected Works of Saint John of the Cross*. Washington, D.C.: ICS, 1973.

_____. *The Collected Works of St. Teresa of Avila*. Two volumes. Washington, D.C.: ICS, 1976.

Liturgy of the Hours. Four volumes. New York: Catholic Book, 1975.

New Catholic Encyclopedia. New York: McGraw Hill, 1967.

Oakes, Edward T. *Pattern of Redemption: The Theology of Hans Urs von Balthasar*. New York: Continuum, 1994.

Schroeder, Gerald L. *The Hidden Face of God: Science Reveals the Ultimate Truth*. New York: Touchstone, 2001.

von Balthasar, Hans Urs. *The Glory of the Lord*, vol. 1. San Francisco: Ignatius, 1982.

Walsh, Michael, ed. *Butler's Lives of the Saints*. Concise edition. San Francisco: Harper & Row, 1985.

NOTES

PART I: *Preliminary Observations*

Chapter One: The Living Pinnacle

1. See Thomas Dubay, *The Evidential Power of Beauty* (San Francisco: Ignatius, 1999), pp. 169–174.

2. See Thomas Aquinas, *Truth*, Robert W. Mulligan, trans. (Chicago: Regnery, 1952), question 1, article 2, p. 11.

3. John of the Cross, *The Dark Night of the Soul,* chapter 19, no. 1, in *Collected Works of Saint John of the Cross,* Kieran Kavanaugh and Otilio Rodriguez, trans. (Washington, D.C.: ICS, 1991), pp. 440–441.

Chapter Two: Antecedents of Holiness

1. John of the Cross, *Spiritual Canticle*, stanzas 14–15, no. 4, in Kavanaugh and Rodriguez, p. 526.

Chapter Three: Basic Attitudes

1. For a detailed program on how to achieve this determination, I suggest my book *Deep Conversion/Deep Prayer* (San Francisco: Ignatius, 2006).

2. *Liturgy of the Hours,* vol. 4 (New York: Catholic Book, 1975), October 19, Feast of Saint John de Brebeuf, pp. 1503–1504.

3. *Liturgy of the Hours,* vol. 4, Monday Morning Prayer, Week II, p. 821.

4. See *Liturgy of the Hours,* vol. 3 (New York: Catholic Book, 1975), Feast of Saint Irenaeus, June 28, p. 1499.

PART II: *The Intercausal Core*

Chapter Four: Transforming Intimacy

1. Waltraud Herbstrith, *Edith Stein: A Biography* (San Francisco: Ignatius, 1971), pp. 64–65.

2. I explain this in *Evidential Power of Beauty*, chapter six, and in chapter seven of this book.

3. *Liturgy of the Hours,* vol. 2 (New York: Catholic Book, 1976), Office of Readings, Friday after Ash Wednesday, pp. 68–69.

4. Bonaventure, *The Soul's Journey Into God*, chapter 7, no. 4, in Ewert Cousins, trans., *Bonaventure* (New York: Paulist, 1978), p. 113.

5. Bonaventure, *Soul's Journey,* chapter 6, no. 3, p. 106.

6. Bonaventure, *Soul's Journey,* chapter 7, no. 6, p. 115.

7. Bonaventure, *Soul's Journey,* chapter 7, no. 5, p. 114.

8. Bonaventure, *Soul's Journey,* chapter 2, no. 8, p. 73.

9. Bonaventure, *The Life of St. Francis,* in Cousins, p. 263.

10. John of the Cross, *The Dark Night,* book 1, chapters 10–11; book 2, chapters 1, 5, 8–12, 17; and *Ascent of Mount Carmel,* book 2, chapter 14, in Kavanaugh and Rodriguez, pp. 381–385, 395–396, 401–403, 409–424, 191–197.

11. See *Deep Conversion/Deep Prayer,* chapters 2–5.

12. See Thomas Dubay, *Prayer Primer: Igniting a Fire Within* (Cincinnati: Servant, 2002), chapters eight and nine, for an introductory treatment of this development and *Fire Within: St. Teresa of Avila, St. John of the Cross, and the Gospel—on Prayer* (San Francisco: Ignatius, 1989) for a much more detailed discussion.

13. See Dubay, *Fire Within,* chapter 11.

14. For a summary of her thought, I suggest you consult Dubay, *Fire Within*, chapter 6.

15. John of the Cross, *Living Flame of Love,* stanza 3, no. 3, in Kavanaugh and Rodriguez, p. 674.

16. Dubay, *Fire Within,* p. 178.

17. John of the Cross, *The Ascent of Mount Carmel,* book 2, chapter 5, no. 6, in Kavanaugh and Rodriguez, p. 117, quoted in Dubay, *Fire Within,* p. 179.

18. John of the Cross, *Living Flame of Love,* stanza 1, no. 3, in Kavanaugh and Rodriguez, p. 642.

19. John of the Cross, *Spiritual Canticle,* stanzas 20 and 21, nos. 1 and 2, in Kavanaugh and Rodriguez, p. 551.

Chapter Five: Heroic Virtue in Action

1. Augustine, *The Trinity,* part I, vol. 5, in John Rotelle, ed., *The Works of Saint Augustine,* Edmund Hill, trans. (New York: New City, 1991), p. 436.

2. Teresa of Avila, *Spiritual Testimonies,* no. 14, in *The Collected Works of St. Teresa of Avila* (Washington, D.C.: ICS, 1987), rev. ed., vol. 1, p. 375.

3. Teresa of Avila, *Soliloquies,* in *Collected Works*, vol. 1, p. 443.

4. Teresa of Avila, *Soliloquies,* pp. 443–460.

5. Teresa of Avila, *Soliloquies,* p. 444.

6. Teresa of Avila, *Soliloquies,* p. 461.

7. Catherine of Siena, "On Divine Providence," in *Liturgy of the Hours,* vol. 2, April 29, Office of Readings, p. 1794.

8. For more in this vein consult the *Catechism* and Henri de Lubac's *The Splendor of the Church* (San Francisco: Ignatius, 1999).

9. Teresa of Avila, *The Book of Her Life,* chapter 33, no. 5, in *Collected Works,* vol. 1, p. 287.

10. Teresa of Avila, Prologue of *The Interior Castle,* no. 3, in *Collected Works*, vol. 2, p. 282.

11. Teresa of Avila, Epilogue of *The Interior Castle,* no. 4; in *Collected Works*, vol. 2, p. 452.

12. Teresa of Avila, *The Interior Castle,* prologue, no. 1, in *Collected Works,* vol. 2, p. 281.

13. *Liturgy of the Hours*, vol. 2, Office of Readings, February 6, pp. 1664–1665.

14. *Liturgy of the Hours,* vol. 3, Office of Readings, February 23, p. 1396.

15. *Liturgy of the Hours,* vol. 4, Office of Readings, August 13, pp. 1313, 1314.

16. See T.F. Casey, "Lourdes," *New Catholic Encyclopedia* (Washington, D.C.: Catholic University, 1967), vol. 8, pp. 1031–1033.

PART III: *Consequences*

Chapter Six: Scriptural Exegetes

1. Hans Urs von Balthasar, *Elucidations* (London: SPCK, 1975), p. 81.

2. Dubay, *Fire Within*, pp. 257–259.

3. Dubay, *Fire Within*, p. 258.

4. A homily by Saint John Chrysostom, in *Liturgy of the Hours,* vol. 2, pp. 68–69.

5. *Liturgy of the Hours,* vol. 4, August 8, Office of Readings, p. 1302.

6. Dubay, *Fire Within*, p. 180, quoting *Spiritual Canticle,* stanza 27, no. 8, in *Collected Works of John of the Cross,* p. 583.

7. Raymond T. Gawronski, "Jesus Christ: Crucified Foundation of the Cosmos," *Communio* 23, no. 2 (Summer 1996), p. 350.

8. *Liturgy of the Hours,* vol. 4, August 20, antiphon at Morning Prayer, p. 1335.

9. Mass and *Liturgy of the Hours*, October 15, translated from the original Latin. These words are inexplicably omitted from the ICEL English rendition.

10. Mass and *Liturgy of the Hours,* December 14, translated from the original Latin. The expression is somewhat weakened in the ICEL English rendition.

Chapter Seven: Marvelous Teachers

1. Hans Urs von Balthasar, *Patristik, Scholastik und wir,* pp. 84–85, cited by Edward T. Oakes, *Pattern of Redemption: The Theology of Hans Urs von Balthasar* (New York: Continuum, 1994), p. 115.

2. Augustine, *The Confessions,* book 10, chapter 27, Maria Boulding, trans. (New York: Random House, 1997), p. 222.

3. This quote is attributed to Saint Augustine, possibly adapted from his *Commentary on St. Matthew,* chapter 6, no. 9.

4. See Dubay, *Deep Conversion/Deep Prayer.*

5. Cited in Joseph Pearce, *Wisdom and Innocence* (San Francisco: Ignatius, 1996), pp. 432–433.

6. Christopher Dawson, "Christopher Dawson's Conversion," *New Oxford Review,* December 1982, p. 9.

7. Von Balthasar, *Elucidations,* p. 81.

8. See Dubay, *Evidential Power of Beauty,* chapter 6, pp. 112–125.

9. Gerald Schroeder, *The Hidden Face of God: Science Reveals the Ultimate Truth* (New York: Touchstone, 2001), p. 51.

10. *National Geographic,* November 2004, pp. 2–35.

11. See Dubay, *Evidential Power of Beauty*, pp. 203–208.

12. Letter from Kelly Olson in "Forum," *National Geographic,* March 2005.

13. Augustine, *The Trinity,* prologue to book 3, chapter 1, no. 2, p. 128.

14. Augustine, *The Trinity,* book 15, no. 51, p. 437.

Chapter Ten: Saints Light Fires

1. Canon 590, no. 2. See Canon Law Society of Great Britain and Ireland, *The Canon Law: Letter & Spirit* (London: Chapman, 1995), p. 326.

2. Augustine, *In Ioannem Tract.,* 32, 8, as quoted in Vatican II, *Optatam Totius,* Decree on Priestly Training, 9; John K. Ryan, trans., *The Confessions of St. Augustine* (New York: Doubleday, 1960), book 10, chapter 27, no. 38, p. 254.

3. Bruno Scott James, *The Letters of St. Bernard of Clairvaux* (Chicago: Regnery, 1953), p. x.

4. See Letter 171 in James, pp. 191–192.

5. G.R. Evans, *The Mind of St. Bernard of Clairvaux* (Oxford: Oxford University Press, 1983), pp. 191, 223.

6. *Liturgy of the Hours,* vol. 4, August 20, antiphon at Morning Prayer, p. 1335.

7. Pope John Paul II, Closing Homily of World Youth Day, August 20, 2000, no. 7, citing Catherine of Siena, Letter 368.

8. See Dubay, *Evidential Power of Beauty*, chapter 11, pp. 209–226.

9. See Dubay, *Evidential Power of Beauty,* especially chapters 3, 4 and 6.

10. For evidence see Dubay, *Prayer Primer,* chapter 9; Dubay, *Deep Conversion/Deep Prayer,* chapter 4; Dubay, *Fire Within*, pp. 212–216.

11. Author's translation.

Chapter Eleven: Icons of Human Love

1. Dubay, *Deep Conversion/Deep Prayer,* p. 70.

2. See *Liturgy of the Hours,* vol. 4, pp. 2016–2018.

Chapter Twelve: Masterpieces of Beauty

1. See Dubay, *Evidential Power of Beauty*, chapter 3.

2. Cited in Gregory Wolfe, *Malcolm Muggeridge: A Biography* (London: Hodder and Stoughton, 1995), p. 338.

3. From a sermon by Saint Bernard of Clairvaux, in *Liturgy of the Hours*, vol. 4, November 1, Feast of All Saints, p. 1526.

4. Lewis Thomas, "On Life in a Hell of a Place," *Discover*, October 1983, p. 42. Cited in Dubay, *Evidential Power of Beauty*, p. 72.

5. Thomas Howard, "Discovering Charles Williams...and the Nuptial Dance," *New Oxford Review*, April 1981, p. 11.

6. Dubay, *Evidential Power of Beauty*, p. 261.

Chapter Thirteen: Glories of Catholicism

1. Herbstrith, pp. 64–65.

2. Ignatius, Letter to the Romans, in Cyril Richardson, ed., *Early Christian Fathers* (New York: Macmillan, 1975), p. 103.

3. *Liturgy of the Hours,* vol. 4, August 13, p. 1314.

4. *Liturgy of the Hours,* vol. 4, August 13, pp. 1313–1314.

5. Teresa of Avila, *Soliloquies,* p. 443.

6. John Vianney, "Act of Love," www.scborromeo.org; see also *CCC,* 2658.

7. *Evidential Power of Beauty,* pp. 113–115, quoting Robert M. Augros and George N. Stanciu, *The New Story of Science: Mind and the Universe* (Lake Bluff, Ill.: Regnery, 1984), pp. 39–40. In this excerpt, Augros and Stanciu quote, in order, from *The Double Helix* (Mentor, 1968), p. 131; and *The Character of Physical Law* (Cambridge, Mass.: MIT Press, 1965) p. 171. For a more complete explanation see Dubay, *Evidential Power of Beauty*, chapter 6, pp. 112–125.

INDEX